Evolution of
Indian Sport Leagues

Evolution of **Indian Sport Leagues:** *The Sport, Media and Management*

Mira K. Desai

KALPAZ

First Published, 2021

Published by

Kalpaz Publications
C-30, Satyawati Nagar,
Delhi – 110052
Ph.: 011-47034999, 9811692060
www.kalpazpublications.com
E-mail: kalpaz@hotmail.com

Printed at: G. Print Process, Delhi

Cataloging in Publication Data—DK
Courtesy: D.K. Agencies (P) Ltd. <docinfo@dkagencies.com>

Desai, Mira K., author.
Evolution of Indian sport leagues : the sport, media and management / Mira K. Desai.
pages cm
Includes bibliographical references.
ISBN 9789353242985 (HB)

1. Professional sports—India—History. 2. Sports teams—India—History. 3. Sports administration—India—History. 4. Sports journalism—India—History. 5. Sports—Economic aspects—India. I. Title. II. Title: Indian sports leagues.

LCC GV653.D47 2021 | DDC 796.0440954 23

In the Memory of

Sumiranand Swami

(ne R.D. Desai)

Newscaster-Ahmedabad Doordarshan
Commentator - Asiad Game 1982
My father who still lives within me

Contents

Post Script

While this book went for print, the Corona virus; Covid-19 Pandemic halted entire world in general and sports business in particular. While IPL 2020 could take place without live audiences in the stadiums, most other events were cancelled or rescheduled. As per the predictions most leagues and other sports matches will not allow audiences at the sports venue in the coming year or so.

The Times of India has carried multiple stories since March 2020 about impact of the pandemic on global sports calendrer. The story on May 30, 2020 lists following two visuals about how pandemic will impact sports league business citing number of people. The assumption is that while major leagues may survive, the minor ones will depend upon their owners.

CORONAVIRUS: MAJOR SPORTS EVENTS AFFECTED

TOI

Tokyo Olympics Postponed to 2021

CRICKET

India-South Africa 2nd ODI in Lucknow & 3rd ODI in Kolkata Cancelled

South Africa tour of Sri Lanka postponed

IPL Suspended until further notice

Australia-New Zealand 2nd ODI in Sydney & 3rd ODI in Hobart Cancelled

PSL Suspended

West Indies tour of England postponed

2021 Women's World Cup qualifiers Postponed

2022 Men's U19 World Cup qualifiers Postponed

ARCHERY

World Cup Shanghai Cancelled

BADMINTON

China Masters Postponed

Asian Team C'ships China and Hong Kong withdrew

German Open Cancelled

Asian Championships Suspended

India Open Suspended

Swiss Open Suspended

Malaysia Open Suspended

Singapore Open Suspended

Thomas and Uber Cup Finals Postponed from May to August 2020

TENNIS

All AITA tournaments Cancelled

BNP Paribas Open Cancelled

Miami Open Cancelled

Monte Carlo Masters Cancelled

French Open Postponed to Sep 20 - Oct 4

Wimbledon 2020 Cancelled

UPDATED ON MAY 12, 2020

Source: The Times of India, AP story May 30, 2020.

While big sports events like Olympics 2020 and number of World Cups have remained postponed or cancelled, it will take minimum three to four years to get back to the routine sports calendar. While beginning of 2021 has started showing signs of revival it is only in the times to come that clear impact of pandemic on sports league business can be analyzed.

While this has impacted the on ground activities, this situation has emerged as an opportunity for the virtual leagues to become stronger due to people being at home. Collaborative games, E-sports, fantasy games, virtual reality games, league formats in other areas is the future of sports league business. OTT platform has started Music League keeping names of State teams of singers. The league business has made competition as core of sports and entertainment above the sporting competence.

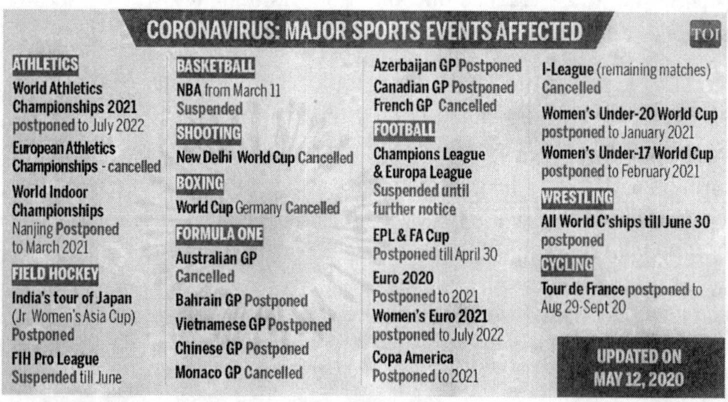
CORONAVIRUS: MAJOR SPORTS EVENTS AFFECTED

TOI

ATHLETICS
World Athletics Championships 2021 postponed to July 2022
European Athletics Championships - cancelled
World Indoor Championships Nanjing Postponed to March 2021

FIELD HOCKEY
India's tour of Japan (Jr Women's Asia Cup) Postponed
FIH Pro League Suspended till June

BASKETBALL
NBA from March 11 Suspended

SHOOTING
New Delhi World Cup Cancelled

BOXING
World Cup Germany Cancelled

FORMULA ONE
Australian GP Cancelled
Bahrain GP Postponed
Vietnamese GP Postponed
Chinese GP Postponed
Monaco GP Cancelled
Azerbaijan GP Postponed
Canadian GP Postponed
French GP Cancelled

FOOTBALL
Champions League & Europa League Suspended until further notice
EPL & FA Cup Postponed till April 30
Euro 2020 Postponed to 2021
Women's Euro 2021 postponed to July 2022
Copa America Postponed to 2021
I-League (remaining matches) Cancelled
Women's Under-20 World Cup postponed to January 2021
Women's Under-17 World Cup postponed to February 2021

WRESTLING
All World C'ships till June 30 postponed

CYCLING
Tour de France postponed to Aug 29-Sept 20

UPDATED ON MAY 12, 2020

Source: The Times of India, AP story May 30, 2020.

The evolution of sport leagues in India and its interconnection with media and management clearly suggest that sports league business was set for next phase of growth, if not for the Pandemic. Yet undoubtedly league business has led to multiple socio-economic changes in the Indian society by inspiring young sporting talent to do well and created culture of sports viewership for games other than cricket.

Sport Leagues are not mere sports but business, finance and socio-cultural shift in the sporting culture of Indian society.

Preface

The idea of this book came mainly because of the success of IPL and other sports leagues that seem to be shaping the future of Indian sporting culture. While league culture is changing the way Indians play and watches the game, interesting development is, the shifting focus from the game to the other aspects and also to games other than cricket in recent times.

This was also an exercise in failed association of academia versus practitioner. As an author it was also a painful experience in bringing together an analysis in the subject area not primarily that of the author. But from a lenses of a researcher, in the interest of the work multiple disciplines that this book is addressing this became an exciting Journey. The decision was to throw the hard work and persistence in darkness or show it the light of the day and for obvious reasons 'light' wins over 'darkness'. Thanks to VDS for this journey!

This was also a lesson in realisation that practice and theory demands critical patience and research rigor to produce such work. While sports get covered regularly by the media, the analysis and reflection on the process of development of the sport scholarship is still at nascent stage in India. Most "Indian" publications related to sports are mainly written by sports journalists or sports commentators and most often either they are the trajectory of events or subjective take on the sporting activity. The material, bringing an analysis of the discipline of sports communication is very limited, in Indian context.

Professional sports league is going to complete 15 years' history in India. This seemingly is the first book that covers the spectrum of professional sports leagues in India and elaborates the intersection of sports with media, business and management. The objective is to help the sports enthusiasts understand the management and those in sports management recognize the media and common reader to understand the spectrum of commercial sports league business. It traces the trajectory of professional sports leagues in India and explores organisational, management, ecological aspects of sports leagues. It is an attempt to help bridge the gap between academia, sports broadcasting and sports management industry. Most material used in this volume is available in public domain and author claims no right to any of it but brings together analysis based on secondary sources.

This book explains global and local similarities and contrasts with reference to sports leagues. This should help sports fan understand the intersection of sports as business, game, technology and its relationship with media, in terms of an administration and management process involving diverse stakeholders.

Mumbai **Mira K Desai**
December 8, 2020

List of Abbreviations

Acronym	: Full Form
2D	: Two Dimensional
3D	: Three Dimensional
AI	: Artificial Intelligence
AIFF	: All India Football Federation
ANOC	: Association of National Olympic Committees
AR	: Augmented Reality
BARC	: Broadcast Audience Research Council
BBC	: British Broadcasting Corporation
BCCI	: Board of Control for Cricket India
CAGR	: Compound Annual Growth Rate
CEDAW	: Convention on the Elimination of All Forms of Discrimination Against Women
CGF	: Commonwealth Games Federation
CSR	: Corporate Social Responsibility
DRS	: Decision Review System
ECB	: England and Wales Cricket Board
EPL	: English Premier League
EY	: Ernst Young
FICCI	: Federation of Indian Chamber of Commerce and Industries
HD	: High Definition
HIL	: Hockey India League

IBL	:	Indian Boxing League
ICC	:	International Cricket Council
ICL	:	Indian Cricket League
IOA	:	Indian Olympic Association
IOC	:	International Olympic Committee
IPL	:	Indian Premier League
ISL	:	Indian Super League
ITU	:	International Telecommunication Union
IYSPE	:	International Year of Sport and Physical Education
KKR	:	Kolkata Knight Riders
KSCA	:	Karnataka State Cricket Association
LNCPE	:	Laxmibai National College of Physical Education
MBL	:	Major League Baseball
MCC	:	Marylebone Cricket Club
NBA	:	National Basketball League
NFL	:	National Football League
NGO	:	Non Government Organisation
NHL	:	National Hockey League
NSNIS	:	Netaji Subhash National Institute of Sports
OCA	:	Olympic Council of Asia
OTT	:	Over The Top
PBL	:	Premier Badminton League
PHL	:	Premier Hockey League
PKL	:	Pro Kabaddi League
PWL	:	Pro Wrestling League
RCB	:	Royal Challengers Bangalore
RIL	:	Reliance Industries Limited
SAI	:	Sports Authority of India
SNIPES	:	National Institutes of Physical Education & Sports
STAR	:	Satellite Television for Asian Region
T20	:	Twenty 20
TNCA	:	Tamil Nadu Cricket Association

TV	:	Television
UEFA	:	Union of European Football Associations
Unesco	:	United Nations Educational, Scientific and Cultural Organisation
USD	:	United States Dollars
UTT	:	Ultimate Table Tennis League
VR	:	Virtual Reality
WWE	:	World Wrestling Entertainment

List of Tables

List of Figures

1

Global-Local of Sports Leagues

*Sports & Society * Sports Administration in India * Sports Leagues * Global Sports Leagues * Sports Leagues in India * Global versus Local League trends.*

Sports, recreation, play, games are terms used to refer to Sports. Sports can be an individual passion, pursuit and pleasure is also an industry, business and entertainment. Sports is not only about players who play sports but is also about those who finance it, govern the processes, those who report and comment on it and even those who deliver sports entertainment. And obviously it is about those who watch, listen or 'consume' it! Sports as a field of studies have diverse disciplinary affiliations.

Sports and Society

Way back in 1970, International Cricket Council (ICC) suspended South Africa from International Cricket indefinitely for its apartheid policy. In 1972, Summer Olympics at Munich West Germany, Palestinian terrorist group Black September took eleven Israeli Olympic team members hostage and killed them along with a West German police officer. In 1980, the then President of United States, Jimmy Carter, led the movement to boycott the Summer Olympic Games in Moscow-Russia, for the Soviet invasion of Afghanistan in December 1979. Closer home, cricket match between India and Pakistan is never a sports event but becomes occasion for patriotic display!

The United Nations Report on The International Year of Sport and Physical Education (IYSPE, 2005) highlighted the importance of Sports for any Society and wellbeing of Humans. Kofi Annan in his message in the report notes, "(sports) values – fitness, fair play, teamwork, and the pursuit of excellence – are universal. At its best, it brings people together, no matter what their origin, background, religious beliefs or economic status. And when young people participate in sports or have access to physical education, they can build up their health and self-esteem, uses their talents to the fullest, learn the ideals of teamwork and tolerance, and be drawn away from the dangers of drugs and crime".

As a discipline, sports aligns with other disciplines as sports sociology, sports psychology, sports nutrition, sports management, sports history, sports diplomacy, sports ethics, sports economics, and so on. Ancient India laid emphasis on skills and competence. Scriptures like *Rig-Veda, Ramayana* and *Mahabharata* provides references to competence in chariot-racing, archery, horsemanship, military tactics, wrestling, weight-lifting, swimming and hunting. A sports study in India is viewed on the line of Physical Education. From school level, physical education is offered as 'optional paper' in school education. Modern Indian society attributes sports with competition and winning unlike ancient Indian society. There are also distinct differences in urban and rural sporting cultures.

Sports and society can be a study of time and space. Leonard Koppett, an American Sports journalist in his 1994 book remarks aptly, "sports reflect, with surprising accuracy, and considerable illumination, societies in which they exist, but they are the mirror and not light. And distorting the mirror won't change what the light shines upon. How societies view sports are indicator of how societies look at time, leisure and values. Meredith Mccleary (2019) remarks that "Going back millennia, pastimes and sports have symbolised societies' values and provided a glimpse into how people spent their free time". He gives examples of Mayans, Medieval kings and cricket in India. The Mayans, some 3500 years back used ball game to determine who will be used for ritual sacrifices. Medieval kings held competitions to show their wealth, allowing the knights to prove their battle prowess and chivalry. Gladiators and even animals were for entertainment by making them compete with each other. In Indian context, there are stories of Aklavya and Arjun and even suitor selected based on skills of archery.

William Morgan in his 2006 book titled *"Why Sports Morally Matters"* brings an interesting examples from American society and highlights that sports can be an interesting space to teach ethics. He brings in analysis, from his own sports and ethics, class, saying that the larger phenomenon of 'growing indifference to moral considerations' is 'writ large in contemporary American sports'. In the Context of South Asia, James Mills in his edited volume of 2005 argues that sports and sporting activities in South Asia have been shaped by exercises in power and resistance and driven by the relationships and forces. He brings together numerous sporting examples that have shaped modern India.

IYSPE (2005) notes that the international community recognised sport as a fundamental right as early as 1959 in the Declaration on the Rights of the Child and then in 1978, the United Nations Educational, Scientific and Cultural Organisation (UNESCO) International Charter of Physical Education and Sport described sport and physical education as a "fundamental right for all". In 1990, the "right of the child to rest and leisure, to engage in play and recreational activities appropriate to the age of the child" was recognised in the Convention on the Rights of the Child (Art. 31). The Convention on the Elimination of All Forms of Discrimination Against Women (CEDAW) of 1979 also affirms that, "on the basis of equality of men and women", women must be ensured "opportunities to participate actively in sports and physical education". A number of other international legal and policy instruments support the right to sport and physical education. However, these instruments have generally received limited weight and the rights to play; sport and physical education have often been described as forgotten rights.

Globally number of agencies use sport in their work, including UNESCO, ILO, the World Health Organisation (WHO), the United Nations Development Programme (UNDP), United Nations Volunteers (UNV), the United Nations Environment Programme

(UNEP), United Nations High Commissioner for Refugees (UNHCR), UNICEF, the United Nations Office on Drugs and Crime (UNODC) and the Joint United Nations Programme on HIV/AIDS (UNAIDS). International Olympics Committee, International Cricket Association and multiple other sports bodies are other professional bodies for global sports coordination.

Sports Administration in India

A sport is a state subject in India. There is Sports Authority of India which maintains stadia, sports infrastructure and looks after sports education. The Ministry of Youth Affairs and Sports, Government of India administers Department of Youth Affairs and Department of Sports in India as two separate secretaries since 2008. It was established in 1982 as Department of Sports for organising IX Asian Games in New Delhi. During 1985, International Year of Youth, it was renamed its present name and became separate Ministry on May 27, 2000. National Youth Policy 2014, Khelo India- National programme for development of sports (https://kheloindia.gov.in/), Sports Authority of India, National Sports University, National Anti-Doping Agency, National Dope Testing Laboratory, Laxmibai National Institute of Physical Education, National Service Scheme, National Yuva Kendra Sangathan, Rajiv Gandhi National Institute of Youth Development are the organisations associated with sports in India.

Each sport in any country has official federation which governs the rules and regulations and venues for that particular sport. National and International games when organised by the Government, sports infrastructures are built up. Subsequently sports authorities come in the existence to maintain those infrastructures. India hosted Asian Games in 1981 which was landmark year for electronic media in India also. In India Sports Authority of India (https://sportsauthorityofindia.nic.in/) came into existence in 1984 under Ministry of Youth Affairs and Sports which has played a significant role in shaping India's sports development by providing training to elite athletes and at the same time operating a number of schemes for identification and development of young talent. The schemes are being implemented through various Regional Centres and training Centres of SAI spread throughout the country.

In India, Sports largely were supported by Indian State and private investment in sports is a recent phenomenon. The government gives grant funding and permissions for national camps and international tournaments only to sports bodies recognised by State. Recently non-government sector has also undertaken sports for gender equality, empowerment, talents search and so on.

The sports federation organises the National Championships, controls sporting arenas, trains the sports persons and provides forum for competitions and training. While block, district, state and national and regional sporting events are common place where 'country' is contesting, sports leagues are example of entry of private players in sports where competition, entertainment and commerce are at the core and not the game per se. National Sports Federations and State Olympic Associations are members of Indian Olympic Association.

Indian Olympic Association (IOA), (https://www.olympic.ind.in/)was formally recognised by Olympic Committee in 1927. It is the governing body for the Olympic Movement and the Commonwealth Games in India. As an affiliated member of the International Olympic Committee (IOC), Commonwealth Games Federation (CGF), Olympic Council of Asia (OCA) and Association of National Olympic Committees (ANOC), the IOA administers various aspects of sports governance and athletes' welfare in the country. Their website remarks that over the years, the IOA undertook wider outreach with several National Sports Federations, and became a governance body that coordinated the sending of multiple sports teams – each selected by their respective National Sports Federations – to the Olympic Games. Later, the IOA also started sending National Teams to Games of the CGF and OCA. KPMG (2016) report notes that most sports federations are controlled by politicians rather than sports people.

In February 2016, sports infrastructure has been given 'industry' status by the government. This will mean private investment as well as more interest in sport management. Sports leagues are also extension of such development. Since otherwise not supported by private players and neglected by the government, sports now are becoming important part of Indian society. India has been planning a *National Sports Development Bill 2011* which was reframed as *Draft National Sports Development Bill 2013* by the Government to bring about reforms in the management and governance of sports to make it "more responsive, responsible and result oriented." Outlook Bureau in its 2017 article noted that there is no clarity about National Sports Legislation which is hanging in air since 2011.Qaiser Mohammad Ali in his January 2020 article traces the trajectory of National Sports Development Code and lists lack of transparent sports administration, will of sporting bodies, political interference as factors impacting effective action in the direction of National Sports Legislation.

The National Sports University Bill 2018 was approved establishing National Sports University in Manipur. In 2019, Sangeeta Nair in her report for Jagran Josh states that the Sports Ministry has constituted 13-member committee to review *Draft National Code for Good Governance in Sports 2017* which has three former athletes of India Anju Bobby George, Bhaichung Bhutia and Gagan Narang. This committee was formed to strike a balance between the autonomy of the National Sports Federations through the accountability and transparency. This committee was to help bring the government and all the stakeholders on the same page for discussion on sports code. The National Code for Good Governance in Sports is basically the universal principles of good governance, ethics and fair play of the Olympic and Sports movement.

Sports Leagues

The potential connection between sports and power was anticipated by the Italian political theorist, Antonio Gramsci (1947/1971) who explained that ruling elites can maintain control over people by sponsoring popular sources of pleasure and excitement. In the modern societies, "Celebrity athletes are drawn into the process of reproducing neoliberal ideas and beliefs when they are hired to endorse corporate products at the same time that they are presented as models for individual success" (Andrews and Jackson, 2001). Sports leagues seem to be an opium for the masses.

Sports leagues are defined as an event where group of teams compete against each other. While in most societies people form sports teams and compete with each other, professional sports leagues are business propositions which are linked with media especially television. There can be variety of sports leagues in industrial societies like University leagues, professional leagues, domestic, leagues, state legue and so on. Roger G Noll and in his 2003 Policy paper referring to sports leagues state that "Teams must agree on the rules of the game, the time and venue at which it will be played, the identity of the officials who will enforce the rules and keep the score, the responsibility for marketing the contest if one objective is to collect revenue, and the procedures for dividing the revenues and costs of the contest".

Globally professional sports leagues are business ventures where apart from sports there is an event around the sport. The teams, on site and off site audiences, advertising and branding in professional leagues is billion-dollar business. Paul A Staudohar and James A Mangan in their edited volume on 'the business of professional sports' (1991) remarks, "Despite proliferation of studies dealing with the history of sports throughout the world in the last decade, little has been written about commercial history of sports" .... they further point that "history, economics and law combine to affect the business of sports, including management, finance, marketing and collective bargaining. The business of sports is what transforms the games into organised entertainment for viewing by a large segment of population. These games provide recreation and diversion but at the same time have a significant impact on socio-culture".

As more general forms of sport participation increasingly depend on private sponsors, the messages associated with sports focus heavily on consumption and the "need" to consume the latest piece of equipment, clothing, or energy drink being endorsed by the athletes. Individually owned franchises, organised together in leagues, unions that represents players in collective bargaining, agents that negotiate individual players' salary, television contracts, government regulations, owners investing into making their teams look attractive, better arenas for the play, satellite rights for television telecast, exhibitions games abroad, foreign franchises, are some of the aspects of sports leagues.

Paul A Staudohar and James A. Mangan (1991) records that professional team sports as packaged events provide considerable entertainment and pleasure for spectators. The success of the sports league is defined by size of on-site as well as off-site spectators. Globally; baseball, basketball, football and hockey leagues are top four followed by Soccer. Whereas in India cricket and kabaddi have done extremely well commercially.

Global Sports Leagues

In industrial societies sports leagues are entertainment and over years there is cultivated league structures, league organisations, fan base. Cain and Haddock in their 2005 paper for *The Journal of Economic History* compares the league histories across USA and England and remark that the peculiarities are "not of a sport but of a shore." The National League of United States was founded in 1876, the first permanent professional team sport league whereas the Football League of England founded 12 years later, was the first in Europe. Cain and Haddock are of the opinion that despite similar economic histories, there are subtle differences in leagues structures across both the countries.

The 'Big Four' of US leagues are- NFL, NBA, MLB and NHL. National Football League (NFL) of America tops any league in the world in terms of global revenue. As per Globalsportsmatters.com, NFL has 29 of the 50 most valuable franchises. It's one hundred and six sports franchises worldwide are valued at more than one billion dollars each and earns profit of millions of dollars every year.

NFL - National Football League (https://www.nfl.com/) was started in 1920. According to Statista, NFL will collect 54.5 billion dollars from TV contracts with Fox (2014-2022), CBS (2014-2022), ESPN (2014-2021) and DirecTV (2015-2022). The Annual Championship of NFL is called *Super Bowl* and it takes place in the first week of February. It is amongst most watched television programme in USA. Fantasy Football like Dream11 (Indian version of fantasy cricket platform) is another way NFL makes money over other professional leagues. DirecTV pays NFL 1.5 billion dollars a year to live stream NFL Sunday Ticket.

NFL 2020 was the 101st season with total 256 games. Usually NFL is played for 17 weeks in a season between September to December of the year. American football is different from European football and closer to the game of rugby which is played both with legs and hands.

MLB - Major Baseball League (https://www.mlb.com/) of USA was the second most revenue earning league in the year 2019. The league generated 10.7 Billion Dollars. It was started in 1903 and it has total 30 city based teams which participate in the league, out of which 15 teams are in the National League and 15 teams in the American league. Apart from 29 teams of USA, one team belongs to neighbouring country Canada. Normal season of MLB runs for around 27 weeks from March to April and September and October in any year.

NBA - National Basketball Association (https://in.nba.com/) is professional basketball league of America. NBA league was started in 1946 and has 29 teams of USA and one team of Canada. Audience of more than 22 million attended 2017-18 game which was 95 percent of arena capacity filled first time. In the 2018-19 season, all 30 NBA teams combined generated the revenues of about 8.76 billion US dollars making this basketball league third wealthiest league in the world. Every year the season starts in October and ends in April.

NHL - National Hockey League (https://www.nhl.com/) is the ice hockey league of USA and it stands fifth in terms of revenues in the world as the league earned revenue of 5.09 Billion Dollars in 2018-19. This league was started in 1917 and has 31 teams participating annually; 24 teams from USA and seven teams from Canada. The season of this 102 years old league runs from October to March every year.

The top leagues for Europe are mainly for football. Spanish La Liga, the English Premier League, the Italian Serie A, and the French Ligue 1 and the German Bundesliga are the main leagues having global following.

- **Spanish La Liga – (https://www.laliga.com/en-GB)** is the Spanish football league with 20 teams. It is the most popular professional league ranked top league of Europe between 2013 to 2019 as per league coefficient rankings by The Union of European Football Association (UEFA). The season of 2018-19 had average attendance of more than 26,000 people.

- **English Premier League– (https://www.premierleague.com/)** is the football league of England and considered as the fourth wealthiest league in the world which earned 7.3 Billion Dollars during 2017-18 Season. The league was found in 1992 and 20 city based teams participate every year. The league season starts from August and runs till May where each team plays 38 matches.
- Serie A – **(http://www.legaseriea.it/en)** is again a football league.
- French Ligue 1 - **(http://www.legaseriea.it/en)** is a French football league.
- German Bundesliga – **(https://www.bundesliga.com/en/bundesliga)** Fußball-Bundesliga or 1. Bundesliga is a German Football League. German Bundesliga is considered to be the toughest league.

Other known global leagues are:

- Australia - ARF - Australian Rules Football
- China- Chinese Professional Baseball League
- Chinese Basketball Association League
- Saudi Professional League – is football league.

Sports leagues have life cycle and therefore there are stories of successes and failures and even closures of the leagues. Apparently Association Football (also known as Soccer) is the most popular game globally which is played by 20 million people in 140 countries as per 2017 data (https://www.factmonster.com).

Sports Leagues in India

The oldest league in India is All India Football Federation (AIFF) *Calcutta Football Club* which was established in 1872 initially as a rugby club and switched to football in 1894 as per the AIFF Website.

The first Indian Football competition and third oldest surviving competition was held in 1888 known as Durand Cup. The oldest Indian club Mohun Bagan was established in 1889 at West Bengal and in 1899 at Thrissur Kerala for football. It was only in 1911 that Mohun Bagan won Indian Football Association's shield which was won by British teams based in India. The *Ranji* Trophy of 1934 is another domestic cricket league which has regional and state cricket associations teams participating annually. The commercial sports league is a twentieth century phenomenon in India.

The commercial sports leagues, as a business, is still at a nascent stage in India. Joy Bhattacharjya in his 2016 article notes about Premier Hockey League, put together by the Indian Hockey Federation, Leisure Sports and ESPN Star Sports in 2005, a good three years before the IPL came around but he notes that after two years of really excellent on field action, India's first professional sports league called it a day due to lack of sponsors and viewership. The next one to start was ISL- Indian Super League which became the Hero Indian Super League (ISL) which kicked off on October 12, 2014. However, the one which got attention and expansion is IPL-Indian Premier League which started in 2008. Subsequent to IPL success, many other leagues have been announced and are in operation in India. Indian Premier League—famous for its pyrotechnics, cheerleaders and huge signing bonuses—had no trouble filling stadiums and attracting TV audiences a decade after its debut as reported by Bhattachariya.

With 800 million people of less than 35 years of age, global sports are an emerging genre of interest for these young audiences in India. Most industry reports as well as sports magazines clearly indicate rise of non-cricketing sports viewership and rise of domestic/professional sports leagues in India. The Indian sports industry is on an upward trajectory breaking new grounds year on year. While cricket proved its dominance in 2019, the industry has doubled its size with CAGR (compound annual growth rate) of 12.8 percent in the business of sports over the last 10 years, cited Vinit Karnik, ESP Properties' business head by the Sportstar 2020 article. In 2020, India has 10 sports leagues including the most successful being Cricket followed by Kabaddi. KPMG (2016) report marks 2008 and 2014 as an important years for sports league business in India; 2008 for the launch of Cricket league and 2014 for multiple other sports leagues. As per industry reports one of the factor contributing to the rise of sports leagues in India is Government intervention.

In 2017, British-Indian entrepreneur Bill Dosing launched two separate leagues; mixed martial arts and boxing in India. He was forced to strike out because India's national boxing federation refused to endorse the tournament. Abhishek Ganguly, MD Puma India has been cited by Amit Bapna in his 2019 article saying "What's important is that there's no one-size-fits-all approach. Some leagues have even failed because they have tried to replicate a commercial model instead of focusing on a sustainable model to build further interest". Tripathy and Kapoor in their 2017 research paper conclude that the factors that impact success of leagues can be broadly summarised into two types: operational factors like league-federation relationship, scheduling and infrastructure; and fan acceptability factors like celebrities, quality of players, marketing communications and match-day experience.

Sports and Media: Newspapers in the history of time announced local sports events and eventually organised sports sections and sports supplements. Sports magazines have considerable market share. With the advent of electronic media, sports broadcasting is one of the essential element of media content scheduling. Mill (2005) in his edited volume argues that spectator converts game into a spectacle rather than a simply a contest between participants….and it is not even necessary to be physically present in the arena, gathering around radio or television sets is an event by itself."

Sporting clashes are now among the most watched and interpreted events in the modern world. Cricket Telecast contract dispute had led to landmark judgment about airwaves as 'public property' in 1995 in India. In 2017, Rupert Murdoch's Star India beat rival bids from Facebook, Sony and India's Airtel to land the IPL's TV and digital rights for five years from 2018. Amit Bapna (2019) attributes factors impacting league consumption to new technologies of snapchat-size formats, social platforms and the exodus to smaller, mobile screens where people also tweet and Swiggy between overs or in half-time of the sporting telecast.

Sports and Brands: In 2019, 329 endorsement deals including 70 new brand endorsement deals took place, of which majority were for cricketers and Virat Kohli and M. S. Dhoni pulled in 63 percent of the total new deals. The non-cricketing brand endorsement space was dominated by women athletes like Badminton world champion P. V. Sindhu, having the most notable being the tie-up with Visa Inc. that made her the first Indian athlete to endorse the financial services brand. Other women athletes are Boxer M. C. Mary Kom, Track and field star Hima Das and Olympic medalist wrestler Sakshi Malik.

Sports, Brands, Media: Marketers want to reach out to audiences using media. The media scenario in India is diverse with thousands of newspapers, hundreds of television channels and multiple languages. In order to reach right audiences, sports are coming to the rescue of the marketers. Sportstar (2020) remarks that while television continue to be the biggest medium for ad spending in sports, the digital medium grew 84 percent year on year to INR 875 crores. The year 2019 also saw fantasy sports applications growing fast as advertisers and this traction will be carried forward into 2020 with new experiences for Indian sports fans. Dream 11 became title sponsor of IPL 2020 making it Dream11 IPL. Brands are building a clear digital plan along with a presence on TV to build a rapport with audiences by reaching out to consumers in multiple ways.

Bapna (2019) in his article quotes Manish Dubey, Chief marketing officer, ICIC Prudential stating that when the power of sport is combined with the latest media accelerators of mobile, data and regional language opens up a whole new world of opportunities for marketers. From branded visibility to engaging local communities, from gamification to branded content, the ways to engage audiences are endless. But, "The sports leagues should go beyond selling air-time and brand logo visibility and create a new generation of multi-axis marketing solutions for customised audience profiles. Then Indian marketers will lap it up," says Manish Dubey.

Global versus Local League Trends

Sports leagues are a nineteenth century occurrence with long history globally but as far as India is concerned it has become commercial only in early twenty first century. The first professional sports league globally is as old as 1876 for Baseball. The National League of Professional Baseball Clubs, popularly known as National League is in United States and Canada having social media fan base running in millions. KPMG 2016 report remarks that while league business is at a nascent stage in India, National Football League of US turned 101 in 2020 and Spain's La Linga will complete 100 years in 2029!

Business Insider in 2019 ranked top ten most valuable sports franchises globally which included nine American and one European. The top five sports leagues in India are Indian Premier League (cricket), Indian Super Leagues (football), Pro Kabaddi League (Kabaddi), Hockey India Leagues (Hockey) and Premier Badminton League (Badminton) as per India Post report of 13 January 2020.

The Indian story of sports league is similar yet different. The Indian journey has its socio-cultural and economic diversities. In 2017, Twenty-two-year-old Nitin Tomar made history in the latest round of player auctions in the Pro League, which is in its fifth season. The young star from a small village in India's north was scooped up for a whopping $145,000, an unprecedented signing fee in the modest world of Kabaddi. The league received a major ring of endorsement in May 2017 when Chinese smartphone giant VIVO signed a five-year sponsorship deal worth nearly $50 million.

Unlike global markets where broad casters make money by subscription, Indian Viewers want to watch sports for free. sports broadcasters in India have to make money through advertisers and sponsors.

In 2005, Adidas- global No. 2 sports brand after Nike, made India hub for Asia business. Adidas India head Andreas Gellnerin has been cited by ET Bureau (2011) article sharing an interesting insight about Indian society and sports. He remarks that India does not look beyond cricket and it's difficult to sell sports gear and accessories yet sports viewership is huge while participation is low. He states that in 2005

Adidas bought over Reebok but "perhaps (India is) the only market where Reebok leads Adidas in sales and revenues. And together they dominate the sports-gear business." His interview has multiple aspects informing about global-local comparison. He says that India is very different from other markets like Japan, Europe and US "where there are many sports and different brands identify with different sports." He further adds Indian consumer approach to fake products as against other countries. He says, "An Adidas consumer in India makes a conscious decision to purchase a counterfeit Adidas product. This is very different from some of the other South-East Asian markets where fake products are very sophisticated… (besides) the north and south preferences in colour and fabric with a different price point makes it a dynamic yet complicated market."

The National Basketball Association (NBA) announced launching professional basketball league in India in January 2020. NBA India representative was cited saying that more than 25 companies have expressed interest in owning the teams. He added, "we are yet to finalise how may teams/franchises should be there. It could be anything between 8 and 12, but currently, it's work in progress…we have also shortlisted 22 arenas." NBA India will be only second after Africa to be outside America.

The future of sports league business in developed countries have saturated and new markets in emerging economies of Asia in general and India in particular undoubtedly provides opportunities for media, marketers, brands, sports people, trainers and coaches, and for many others. It provides entertainment to audiences and creates sports culture in the society. It also brings with it side effects of drugs, betting, sex scandals and corruption. Yet there is no doubt that sports leagues in India have many more decades to grow and these early decades indeed were very eventful which has been covered in this volume.

Another aspect which needs to be recognised is sociological-Indian joint families and festivals; be it religious or cultural, keeps people busy. League business has provided alternative modes of entertainment and recreation to increasing nuclear families of urban India which reside in urban cities and television or mobile based entertainment to people in towns and villages who too travel specially to watch ongoing league matches mainly to talk about it in their social circles.

Leaving league as entertainment, about Indian Sporting Cultures, ***Qaiser Mohammad Ali in his January 2020 article for Outlook India notes a dramatic closure;*** "The American swimmer won 28 Olympic medals, including 23 gold. India has a grand total of nine gold, in a total of 28, in 119 years of Olympic participation. All arguments end there."!

2

Dawn of the Cricket League

*[Trajectory of Cricket in India * Beginning of Cricket Leagues * IPL Journey * IPL Scandals & Controversies * Economics of IPL * Sponsors * IPL in 2020 * IPL and Allied Benefits for Team Owners * IPL & Sports Business]*

Leagues are professional private ventures where team sports and television (now digital media) intersects in order to reach out to multiple audiences- onsite as well as offsite; physical as well as broadcast/digital audiences. Since cricket is another religion in India, it was probably obvious that the private leagues in sports will begin with the game of cricket only. But interestingly enough the first league to start in India was not cricket, it was Hockey. It is another story that cricket league made league business more profitable and acceptable to Indian society eventually.

Trajectory of Cricket in India

The website of Board of Control of Cricket in India (BCCI) traces the beginning of cricket in India to the year 1721 (https://www.bcci.tv/about/history) and the first recorded cricket match between the British army and the English settlers in 1751. The formation of the first Cricket Club in the country was at Calcutta (now Kolkata) in 1792 (now known as Calcutta Cricket and Football Club- CC & FC) which is the second oldest in the world after Marylebone Cricket Club (MCC) in England in 1787 (which is since 1814 is based at Lord's cricket ground at London). Parsis and Princely states can be credited with the growth of the game of cricket in the country.

The year 1911 witnessed the first-ever tour of England by an 'All-India' team which was sponsored and captained by the Maharaja of Patiala featuring the best cricketers of that time. In a meeting held at the Bombay Gymkhana on 10th December 1927 decided with a unanimous decision to form a 'Provisional' Board of Control to represent cricket in India and in late 1928, six cricket associations were formed in India- Southern Punjab Cricket Association, Cricket Association of Bengal, Assam Cricket Association, Madras Cricket Association and Northern India Cricket Association. It is in 1929 that International Cricket Council (ICC) recognised India but the recognition as test playing nation came in 1932 and Bombay (now Mumbai) became the base for BCCI. BCCI has ten cricket grounds in the country with the seating capacity in the range of 25000 at Vishakhapatnam and Dharamshala to 80,000 at Eden Gardens Kolkata. Eden Garden in Kolkata is the largest cricket stadium in the country and third largest in the world.

Beginning of Cricket Leagues

Globally in 1976 Australian media tycoon Kerry Packer started World Series Cricket (WSC) by signing top cricketers to play for his television channel; Channel 9 because he lost on the telecast rights of Test Matches in Australia. WSC, writes Rajesh Tiwary (2017) changed the face of the game in many ways; coloured dresses, day-night games, helmets, fielding restrictions, and many other things that are an essential part of the modern game were either first introduced in WSC, or were made popular by it. In 2003, Twenty20 (T20) cricket was introduced in England and branded by England and Wales Cricket Board (ECB) as the carnival of cricket. The format became an instant hit drawing huge crowds at every venue. Within next couple of years, Australia, New Zealand and South Africa introduced T20 cricket as part of their domestic season. In 2007, T20 cricket's first international tournament, World T20, was formalised by the International Cricket Council (ICC).

During 2007 to 2009 Zee Group introduced the concept of Indian Cricket League (ICL) for cricket. Rajesh Tiwary in his article for First Post in 2017 remarks, "ICL is a faint memory in the minds of those who followed the game. It's hard to find video clips or scorecards for the tournament on the internet. Cricket pundits on TV never talk about it. It's almost as if the league never existed. It's occasionally brought up during match-fixing trials and allegations of corruption". He further notes, "ICL's significance in bringing professionalism to India's domestic cricket structure cannot be denied. One of the first impacts of ICL even before the league actually started was BCCI revising pay structure for domestic players in an attempt to prevent them from breaking away. ICL was also the precursor to IPL, the world's biggest cricket tournament right now in terms of the sums of money involved". Pande (2012) remarks that the Indian Cricket League (ICL), promoted by Zee, died because it did not have a buy in from the Indian board (*BCCI*) that runs cricket in India and so could not draw the best of the current players.

Shankkar Aiyar (2008) describes the trajectory of Lalit Kumar Modi and his company in starting the cricket league. His company Modi Entertainment Network entered into a joint venture with US-based API Sponsorship for a new cricket league with the idea to draw up a business proposition with sportscaster ESPN. He signed up players and created Teams-Mumbai Stallions, Calcutta Tigers, Bangalore Braves, Hyderabad Hawks and, to please Scindia, Gwalior Cobras which did not work out. The threat of a competing league hosted by Zee's Subhash Chandra and convincing by Lalit Kumar Modi created the BCCI backed Cricketing League by October 2007 and the rest, as they say, is history!

The then BCCI Vice President Lalit Kumar Modi, Chairman & Commissioner for IPL started with the 80 top ICC-ranked players from nine countries. Then he got down to the scheduling. The broadcast rights for India and abroad were sold for $1.02 billion (4,080 crores)-including $108 million (432 crores) in promotions-for 10 years. A prospectus was drawn up and 14 Corporates entered the fray, eight of whom bagged a team each. Shankkar Aiyar (2008) has done a cover story about ownerships of IPL Teams and brings insights about how team owners are associated with BCCI and how their business interests and cricketing passion is impacted their economic and personal decisions. The story titled 'Lord of League' keeps a headline about how 14 years' journey of Lalit Kumar Modi culminated into a scale of success.

The League involved carting 1,000 people-eight teams, nearly 700 BCCI officials and 100 representatives of sponsors- across the country every day. In its first season over 44 days, 12,000 hotel room nights and 20,000 air tickets were logged in by IPL. "There was no way we were going to allow a team to be late. So we tied up with ITC for accommodation and Kingfisher for flights," Lalit Modi was cited saying in the article by Aiyar.

IPL Journey

The IPL (Indian Premier League) is the first professionally run sports league in India which has become financially viable after a while. All the well-known cricketers are associated with this league. It has been considered as World's top 10 profit making league by the experts. IPL completed 13 seasons by November 2020. The amount of money which is associated with the league can be gauzed by the prize at which its global media rights were sold. It was broadcast on Star sports and Star has bought the global media rights of IPL at around 944 million USD for a period of Five years in the year 2018. Table 2.2 lists all the seasons of IPL from 2008 to 2020.

Table 2.1: IPL Seasons over the years

Season	*Opening Ceremony Date/ Venue*	*Total Teams*	*Calendar /Match Days#*	*Total Matches Scheduled*	*Total Matches Played*	*Finals Date*	*Place of Finals*	*Winner*
S1	18 April 2008	8	45/44	59	59	1 June 2008	Navi Mumbai	Rajasthan Royals
S2	18 April 2009	8	37/37	59	57 (Rain)	24 May 2009	South Africa	Deccan Chargers
S3	12 March 2010	8	45/43	60	60	25 April 2010	Mumbai	Chennai Super Kings
S4	8 April 2011	10	51/49	74	73 (Rain)	28 May 2011	Chennai	Chennai Super Kings
S5	4 April 2012	9	54/51	76	74 (Rain)	27 May 2012	Chennai	Kolkata Knight Riders

(Contd...)

S6	2 April 2013/ Kolkata	9	54*/50	76	76	26 May 2013	Kolkata	Mumbai Indians
S7	15 April 2014/UAE	8	48*/41	60	60	1 June 2014	Bangalore	Kolkata Knight Riders
S8	7 April 2015/Kolkata	8	48*/44	60	57 (Rain)	24 May 2015	Kolkata	Mumbai Indians
S9	9 April 2016/ Mumbai	8	51/48	60	60	29 May 2016	Bangalore	Sunrisers Hyderabad
S10	5 April 2017/Multiple Ceremonies	8	47/43	60	59 (Rain)	21 May 2017	Hyderabad	Mumbai Indians
S11	7 April 2018	8	51/48	60	60	27 May 2018	Mumbai	Chennai Super Kings
S12	23 March 2019	8	51/48	60	60	12 May 2019	Hyderabad	Mumbai Indians
S13	2020	8	46/46	60	60	10 November 2020	Dubai, UAE	Mumbai Indians

* Including Opening Ceremony

Calendar days will be less as the multiple matches took place on single day.

Source: Compilation by Author based on various sources.

IPL is unique in more than one ways:

1. IPL became first commercial cricket league of India which has become successful.
2. IPL was the first sporting event to have been broadcast live on YouTube in 2010.
3. IPL was the second highest-paid league, based on first-team salaries on a pro-rata basis, only second to NBA league.
4. DLF (Delhi Land & Finance) paid around $50 million to secure the title sponsorship for the first three years.
5. 9,000 crores rupees is the worth of the IPL including teams and sponsors. The size of the cricket economy is 4,800 crores which rose by 50% post-IPL.
6. The inaugural IPL had Winner's Prize money of 48 million which became 500 million by 2019 and 2020 due to Pandemic total prize money was reduced by half.
7. In 2008, there were 163 players in IPL of which 96 Indians and 67 foreigners. The number became 187 players with 125 Indians and 62 foreign players in 2020.

8. Usually international cricket is played in nation versus nation format but IPL bring in domestic competitions like Mumbai versus Delhi or Punjab versus Bangalore.

Table 2.2 shows how owners and teams of IPL have changed over the years and teams have been discontinued also. In IPL, a franchise owns a cricket team, most owned by Business families and Bollywood celebrities. One of the franchise; Chennai Super Kings became public limited company in 2014. The website of Chennai Super Kings Cricket Limited (www.chennaisuperkings.com) notes, "The Company arranges cricket matches, as well as retails jersey and t-shirts, mugs and wall posters, footwear, wrist bands, and other accessories", clearly indicating other modes of doing business.

Table 2.2: IPL Teams and Owners

No	*Name of the Team*	*Year of Inception*	*First Owners*	*Main Owners in 2020*
1.	Pune Warriors India	2011	Sahara Group	Team does not exist
2.	Kochi Tuskers Kerala	2011	Anchor Earth and Parinee Developers	Team does not exist
3.	Mumbai Indians	2008	Reliance Industries Limited	Reliance Industries Limited
4.	Royal Challengers Bangalore	2008	Vijay Mallya & UB Group	Diageo through United Spirits Limited
5.	Deccan Chargers Hyderabad (Now new Name- Sunrisers Hyderabad with new Owners)	2008	Deccan Chronicle Holding Ltd. (DCHL)	Team Renamed from 25 October 2012 owned by Sun TV Network
6.	Chennai Super Kings	2008	India Cements	Chennai Super Kings Cricket Ltd
7.	Delhi Dare Devils (Now new Name- *Delhi Capitals*)	2008	GMR Group	GMR & JSW Sports (Jindal South West Sports) 50%-50%
8.	Kolkatta Knight Riders	2008	Shahrukh Khan, Jay Mehta and Juhi Chawla	Red Chillies Entertainment (55%) & Mehta Group
9.	Kings XI Punjab	2008	Mohit Burman (Dabur India), Ness Wadia (Wadia Group), Preity Zinta & Karan Paul (Apeejay Surendera Group)	Mohit Burman (46%) Ness Wadia (23%) Preity Zinta (23%) Karan Paul (8%)

(*Contd...*)

10.	Rajasthan Royals	2008	Jaipur IPL Cricket Pvt. Ltd, Kuki Investments Ltd (Raj Kundra and Family-11.7 % share)	Amisha Hathiramani(Tresco International Ltd)- 44.2%, Manoj Badale (Emerging Media (IPL) Ltd)- 32.4%, Lachlan Murdoch (Blue Water Estate Ltd)- 11.7% , Shane Warne- 3 %

Source: Compilation by Author based on various sources.

Like any other sports league, in IPL teams are owned by the franchise owner who can acquire a player in five ways: by the annual auction, buying domestic players, signing uncapped players, through trading and buying replacements. In the trading window the player can only be traded with his consent.

Some of the IPL Team composition rules are:

- Minimum squad strength of 16 players plus one physio and a coach.
- No more than 10 foreign players in the squad and at least four foreign players should be there in each squad.
- Minimum of eight local players must be included in each squad.
- A minimum of two players from the BCCI under-22 pool in each squad.

Some of the differences of IPL to international Twenty-20 (also known as T20i) cricket:

- While T20i global teams participate, IPL has only local teams with few foreign players.
- There is a difference in a timeout. It gives the players an opportunity to strategize and take a drink during the strict 2 minutes, 30 seconds time limit. Each team is awarded two timeouts per innings totaling to four timeouts for the whole game. The teams can take the timeout when instructed, but it is necessary to take it from 6th to 9th and 13th to 16th overs.
- IPL is also known for having commercials during the game. However, there may be a penalty if the umpires find teams misusing this privilege at their own choice.

- Pakistani cricketers cannot participate in IPL since 2009 due to reasons not clearly stated.

Teams and Matches: In the current form of the IPL tournament format, each of the eight teams play with another seven teams twice making total of at least 14 matches for each team in every season. After the 14 matches, top four teams of the points table qualify for the play offs. Play offs are designed in such a manner that the winning team directly goes to the final match but losing team of the first play-off game gets another chance to prove their capability and in the same manner winning team of the second playoff game have to play another game to prove their mettle and in this way second team for the final match is decided. In 2014, due to controversies interim officials were installed, Sunil Gavaskar was asked to head IPL and Shivlal Yadav was asked to head BCCI and N Srinivasan was told to step down. In twelfth season new Concussion rules were introduced in the test format.

Venue of Matches: The IPL timetable have at times clashed with the Indian General Election leading to the shifting of the IPL Venues outside India. In 2009, with attack on Sri Lankan Cricketers in Pakistan in March 2009 led to shifting of the IPL S2 to South Africa. The reasons cited were concerns regarding players' security. In Third Season Deccan Chargers did not play at Hyderabad due to ongoing political crisis for Telangana region. Third Season also added Nagpur and Cuttack as new bases for the tournament. Even over the years' venues are changed due to varied reasons. As evident from the Table 2.1, IPL moved outside India thrice (from its inception up to 2020); to South Africa in 2009, to United Arab Emirates in 2015 and again in 2020. IPL 2020 was played outside India at three venues in UAE-Dubai, Sharjah and Abu Dhabi. Except for Covid-19 pandemic conditions usually IPL is played during April to May every year. IPL 2020 was played during 19 September to 10 November 2020.

Player Auctions: Srinivas and Vivek in their 2009 book on IPL note that the two auctions of 2008 and 2009 for foreign players after the first season of IPL has clearly proved that IPL was not at all about cricket but about commercial interests of franchise owners, players and BCCI. The S2 auction was held in Goa with all glamour and glitz for 50 foreign players on 6 February 2009 which was aired live on television. IPL 2020 auction was held in December 2019 at Kolkata and was live streamed on Hot Star App and news site of Star Sports Network.

IPL Scandals and Controversies

There have been numerous controversies associated with the IPL especially between 2009 to 2013 where media covered cases by the Central Bureau of Investigation (CBI), the Enforcement Directorate (ED) and the involvement of politicians leading to the game of cricket taking a back seat. Many of these are Court cases under judicial consideration and therefore prohibited from public discussion. The author merely lists some of the controversies in the interest of readers to recognize nature of controversies and do not intend to interfere with the process of justice.

In 2009, Lalit Modi, the then Commissioner of IPL lost presidential election in Rajasthan Cricket Association, criminal charges were filed against him in Rajasthan. In 2010 at the IPL fourth season, the bid around the Kochi franchisee turned controversial resulting in the resignation of the then Union Minister, Shashi Tharoor and investigations by various departments of the Government of India into the financial dealings of IPL and the other existing franchisees.

On July 20, 2011, the Enforcement Directorate (ED had issued show-cause notices to Modi and the BCCI under provisions of Foreign Exchange Management Act (FEMA) regarding a bank account opened in South Africa by the BCCI ahead of the IPL cricket tournament in 2009. Modi was expelled from the BCCI in 2010, who accused him of rigging bids and money laundering among other charges. He, however, refused to let go of his position in the Rajasthan Cricket Association (RCA), prompting the BCCI to altogether ban the association.

In October 2010, the Rajasthan Royals and Kings XI Punjab had their franchises terminated for breaching the ownership rules. Two months later both teams were finally allowed to take part in the 2011 edition after a court ruling. The new Kochi franchise was also issued a warning to resolve all their ownership disputes and eventually could not play IPL.

The May 2013 IPL match fixing scandal not only impacted IPL, but also to the game of cricket in India. During IPL S6 three cricketers of Rajasthan Royals were supposed to have links with bookies and received money to fix matches for IPL. In 2014, India TV sting operation led to banning and suspension of five domestic cricketers. In 2015, Indian Express newspaper did a story about Lalit Modi having ownership stakes in three IPL franchises. On 14 July 2015, BBC News (https://www.bbc.com/news/world-asia-india-33517583) carried a story about banning of Rajasthan Royal and Chennai Super Kings for two years and banning of Raj Kundra and Gurunath Meiyappan for life by Supreme Court of India. These teams were found guilty for illegal betting and match fixing wrongdoings during 2013 tournament.

In April 2016, Bombay High Court ruled out some matches of IPL tournament to be moved out of State of Maharashtra. Thirteen matches scheduled during May 2016 at Mumbai, Pune and Nagpur had to be moved out of the State to 'Save Water' as Maharashtra monsoon had failed for previous two years. Vivek Kaul in his 2016 book titled *India's Big Government* elaborates the water controversy associating with IPL and notes, "this was a classic case of a scapegoat being found and the real 'culprit' getting scot-free". He is of the opinion that by involving IPL in water shortage was mainly to divert attention from real reasons behind water scarcity debate in Maharashtra!

Anand Vasu (2019) does a critical piece on status of cricket administration in India with multiple examples including one about Rupa Gurunath who has been elected president of Tamil Nadu Cricket Association in September 2019. She is the daughter of Former ICC Chairperson, BCCI former Chief, India Cement as well as Chennai Super Kings Owner N Srinivasan, and wife of Gurunath Meiyappan who is serving life ban for his involvement in 2013 IPL scandal. Vasu shares that on August 13, 2017 Lalit Modi resigned from Rajasthan Royals, resigned as President of the Nagpur District Association, ending his presence in the Rajasthan Cricket body, which was banned by the BCCI.

Many times judicial committees had to intervene and point out irregularities which were going on in the IPL. In 2015, Justice Mudgal Committee and in 2016 Justice Lodha Committee underlined multiple irregularities in the administration of the cricket league leading to changes in cricket administration in the country. But its widely accepted fact that IPL is big money and glamour and it's a globally accepted successful league from India.

Economics of IPL

While limited details about financial transactions can be authenticated, following are the main sources of revenue for IPL which is based on publically available material.

Broadcasting Rights: A consortium consisting of India's Sony Entertainment Television network, and Singapore-based World Sport Group, secured the global broadcasting rights of the IPL for ten years at a cost of US $1.026 billion on 15 January 2008. As part of the deal, the consortium paid the BCCI US $918 million for the television broadcast rights and US $108 million for the promotion of the tournament. This deal was challenged in the Bombay High Court by IPL, and got the ruling on its side. After losing the battle in court, Sony Entertainment Television signed a new contract with BCCI with Sony Entertainment Television paying ₹ 8,700 crore (US$1.93 billion) for 10 years.

Sony-WSG then re-sold parts of the broadcasting rights geographically to other companies. On 4 March 2010, ITV announced it had secured the United Kingdom television rights for the 2010 Indian Premier League. ITV televised 59 of the 60 IPL matches on its ITV4 free to air channel. On April 1, 2011, Rogers Sportsnet announced that it signed a four-year exclusive deal in Canada to broadcast 36 group stage matches, 3 playoff matches and one championship match on Rogers Sportsnet One. In 2020 IPL S13, three categories of rights were put on sale by the BCCI – global television rights and rest of the world digital rights (GTVRD), digital rights for the Indian subcontinent alone (ID), and the global consolidated rights comprising worldwide TV and digital rights (GCR). As was the case with the Indian Premier League, if the globally consolidated bid exceeds the sum of the GTVRD and ID, then that bid wins. If not, the individual bids – India television + global digital and India digital rights will be deemed winners. BCCI media rights auction stands at ₹ 60.32 billion, which amounts to ₹ 591 million per match as per Business Standard December 2019 report, up from ₹ 430 million per match paid by star India.

Sponsorship Rights: The IPL had signed up Kingfisher Airlines as the official umpire partner for the first Season for ₹ 106 crores (US$23.53 million and approximately £15 million) deal for five years. This deal saw the Kingfisher Airlines brand on all umpires' uniforms and also on the giant screens during third umpire decisions. Vijay Mallya has IPL team Bangalore Royal Challengers as a marketing platform for his own brands and his brand is also on T-shirts of four other IPL teams.

India's property developer DLF Group paid US$50 million to be the title sponsor of the tournament for three years from 2008 to 2010. A spot in the limelight and embedded advertising for DLF gave them billing every time a six was hit. Other year sponsorship agreements include a deal with motorcycle maker Hero Honda worth $22.5 million, one with PepsiCo worth $12.5 million, and a deal with beer and airline conglomerate Kingfisher at $26.5 million. In 2010, the IPL had 80 official merchandising deals. It has signed a deal with Swiss watchmaker Bandelier to make official watches for the IPL.

Teams such as Shah Rukh Khan's (SRK) Kolkata Knight Riders (KKR) have roped in professional CEOs with experience in financial services to bolster their chances of success and find a way out of cricketing mediocrity. KKR ended third—from the bottom-on the ground; but with an array of sponsors, they had deals worth Rs 45 crores in the first year. SRK attempted everything from cutting a music album deal with T-Series to a merchandising deal with Reebok, which opened the first RBK Knight Riders store in Kolkata. When KKR put its shirts on sale, Reebok's store at Linking Road in Mumbai sold 400 T-shirts on the first day, driven by SRK's Pan-Indian appeal.

Mobile applications: DCI Mobile Studios (A division of Dot Com Infoway Limited), in conjunction with Sigma Ventures of

Singapore, have jointly acquired the rights to be the exclusive Mobile Application partner and rights holder for the Indian Premier League cricket matches worldwide for the next eight years (including the 2017 season). Recently, they have released the IPL T20 Mobile applications for iPhone, Nokia Smart phones and Blackberry devices.

Official website: The IPL negotiated a contract with the Canadian company Live Current Media Inc. to run and operate its portals and the minimum guarantee has been negotiated at US $50 million over the next 10 years. The official website of the tournament is www.iplt20.com. Incorporating popular forms of social media into the third season of the IPL, the website now contains a more holistic presence across all online mediums. The website apart from featuring new additions to empower user interaction, has encouraged a wider range of websites around IPL like, IPL Tracker and IPL Mag amongst other more traditional reporting websites.

Ticketing: Apart from off site, on site audience is another source of revenue. Federal Bank, a major Indian commercial bank in the private sector, with headquarters in Aluva, Kerala, was the principal sponsor of Kochi Tuskers Kerala (KTK). The tickets for KTK's home matches were sold through Federal Bank branches and their website. The Ticket sales of Kochi Tuskers Kerala was officially started in a ceremony hosted at the Le Meridian Hotel Kochi, on March 28. Soon after, the tickets become available at the teams official ticketing partner website kyazoonga.com. Given the 80,000 capacity of Eden Garden, KKR would have made ₹ 2.5 crores per match.

Comic Books: The Chennai Super Kings Captain with his team mates featured in a comic book series specifically targeting the team's young fans. The 40-page book priced 40 each with an initial print run of 40,000 copies hit the stands coinciding with the start of the Indian Premier League S4. Mumbai-based advertising company Cartwheel Creative Consultancy Pvt. Ltd produced the series. It tied up with India Book House for nationwide distribution of the comics. Even for IPL S5 Puma, sponsor of two teams- Rajasthan Royals and Deccan Chargers released player autographed two comic features called 'Rock 'n' Royals' and 'Electric Chargers'.

Global following: IPL S3 saw fan following in the United Kingdom, mainly because telecasts being moved from the subscription-based Setanta Sports to the free-to-air ITV4. In 2018, IPL was telecast in Australia and New Zealand and same year also witnessed Over The Top (OTT) viewership for sports entertainment. Hotstar (OTT platform) set a world record of 10.7 million concurrent viewers beating 2012 record of 8 million concurrent viewers. The 2020 season witnessed surge of 30 percent in the viewership also due to lock down. IPL has fan following globally and digital platforms makes it possible for audiences to reach out irrespective of geography. The digital broadcasts also make it possible for Indian diasporas globally to renew their love of game, cricketers and Bollywood with many team owners being in the stands.

The 2020 season used four large virtual fan walls with pre-recorded videos of cheerleaders on branded walls of sponsors. IPL teams like Mumbai Indians and Rajasthan Royals launched digital initiatives to connect with fans. Mumbai Indians launched 'MI Live' and 'Paltan Play' and Rajasthan Royals ran a community-based programme called 'Super Royals'. Due to Pandemic in 2020 IPL lost out on onsite audience revenue.

Valuation of IPL

Table 2.3 elaborates the growth in terms of valuation of IPL and viewership over the years. IPL ecology involves players, spectators, owners, sponsors and alliance of cricket, entertainment, business and media. Everyone except the spectator is in it for making money. The Economic Times commissioned UK-based Brand Finance to carry out brand evaluation of the IPL and each of the eight franchise teams (numbered 10 in 2011). IPL was valued at US $4.13 billion (18,998 crores) in 2010 double than its value of US $2.01 billion in 2009 by the same consultancy. In 2011, the valuation pegged at nearly US $3.7 billion, decline due to corruption and other scandals. Gurav Gupta in his 2018 article in *The Times of India* cites Duff & Phelps, global valuation and corporate finance advisers, Report stating that after 11th Season IPL valuation has seen 19 percent jump amounting to US $ 6.3 billion. Social media is another marker of brand value.

While 2017 Season garnered 642,900 mentions the number grew to 855,400 in 2018 season and became 1.3 million after two weeks.

Table 2.3: IPL Valuation and Reach across Seasons

Season	*Year*	*Valuation by Brand Finance (in $ Billions)*	*Total Viewership (in Millions)*
1.	2008	-	102.4
2.	2009	2	122.7
3.	2010	4.13	143.7
4.	2011	3.67	162
5.	2012	2.92	163
6.	2013	3.03	170
7.	2014	3.25	174 / 552 (KPMG, 2016)
8.	2015	3.54	49.4
9.	2016	4.16	121
10.	2017	5.3	363.9 (1.25 billion Impressions)
11.	2018	6.3	769 (1.434 billion Impressions)
12.	2019	6.7	490 (BARC Rating)
13.	2020	700 million to 1 billion USD (Estimated Losses)	31.57

Source: Compilation by author based on varied sources listed in Bibliography.

Apart from the season valuation, the Team valuations are also another aspect for IPL valuation. One analyst remark that the four teams out of the eight made a profit in 2009. Chennai Super Kings was rated in 2011 "the most valuable team" in Indian Premier League cricket, with a brand value of US$ 48.4 million (app. ₹ 224 crores), 2.4 million more than Kolkata Knight Riders, of which brand value stood at US $46 million. The brand value of Mumbai Indians and Chennai Super Kings shot up to US $57 million and US $55 million respectively in 2011. There are disputed figures for the profitability of the teams. While the *London Times* said that all but Kings XI Punjab made a profit in the S4. The team valuations too change year after year. Gaurav Laghate in his September 22, 2019 story for *The Economic Times* cites Mumbai Indian as top franchise and CSK second that returned to IPL in 2018 after two-year ban imposed in 2015. Figure 2.1 based on Duff & Phelps IPL Brand Valuation Report 2019 shows how Mumbai Indians, champions of IPL, has continuous rise in its valuation.

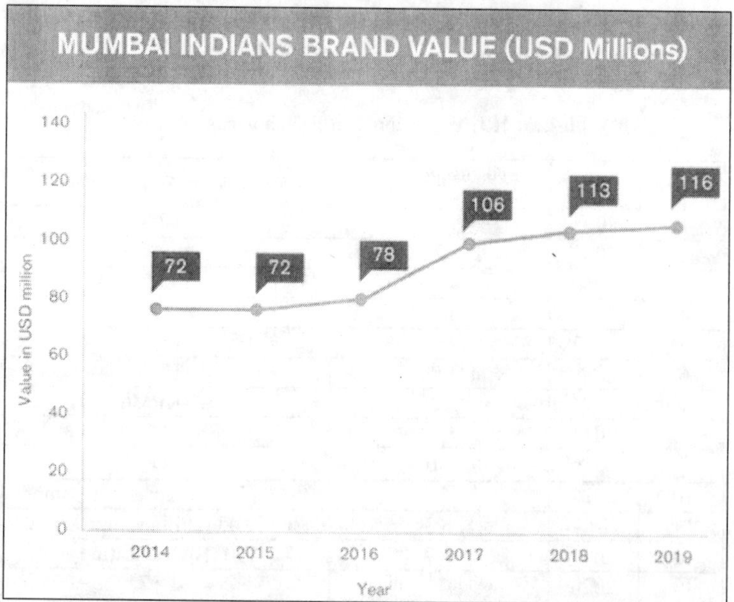

Source: https://www.socialsamosa.com/2020/09/ipl-brand-collaborations-2020/ from Duff & Phelps IPL Brand Valuation Report 2019

Figure 2.1: Valuation of Mumbai Indians over the years.

Sponsorships

Sportstar in its March 2020 article notes the rise in sports sponsorship to ₹ 9,000 crore citing ESP Properties Report. The article provides figure of 17 percent rise a year and suggest that on-ground sponsorship has grown 25 percent and crossed ₹ 2,000 crores in a year for the first time. On sale are spots—on jerseys, shoes and sleeves—the rates for which range from 3 crores to 25 crores. Rakesh Singh, marketing manager of Chennai Super Kings says "The best part about the IPL is that you get paid for almost everything."

Figure 2.2 shows how varied sectors have associated themselves with IPL as sponsors across eight IPL teams. There are no clear patterns across teams yet there are 12 sponsorship categories for 2019 season ranging from type of sponsors to nature of products sponsoring the teams. Gaurav Laghate (2020) in his story about sports sponsorship comments that the endorsement industry grew by 11% to ₹ 537 crores where cricketers contributed the most. Almost 85% of total brand endorsements have come from cricketers, and Virat Kohli and MS Dhoni cornered 63% of the total brand endorsements. In 2019, total of 329 endorsement deals took place out of which 228 brands signed up with cricketers.

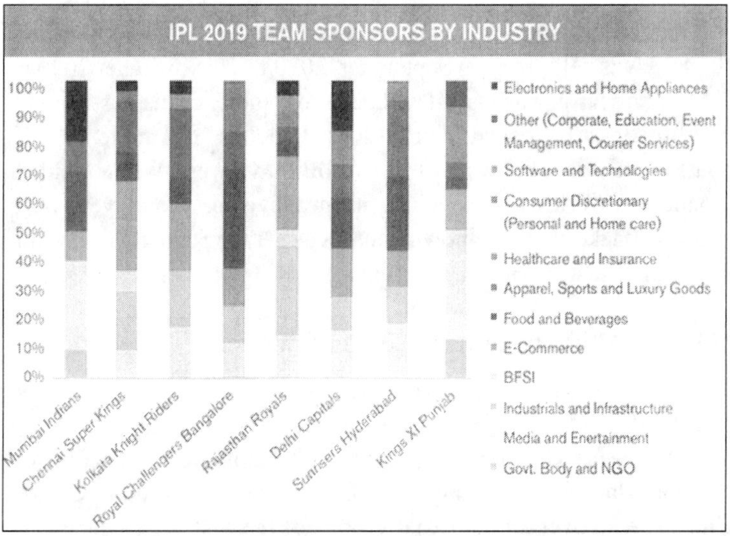

Source: https://www.socialsamosa.com/2020/09/ipl-brand-collaborations-2020/ from Duff & Phelps IPL Brand Valuation Report 2019

Figure 2.2: IPL 2019 Sponsors sectors.

It is necessary to understand the difference of terms like advertisers, clients, owners, management, sponsors, sports persons, brands, and broadcasters. All of them play important roles in organizing and managing the sports league business.

IPL in 2020

The IPL was scheduled to begin from March 29, 2020 but the tournament had to be postponed initially until April 15 due to the coronavirus pandemic. At the time of BCCI's announcement, the Central Government had also suspended all visas to India till April 15 as part of measures to contain the spread of the virus. Duff & Phelps, the multinational financial consultancy firm estimated decline in the value of the IPL ecosystem by US $700 million to US $1 billion. Business Today claimed that if 2020 games were cancelled altogether, it would costed have the BCCI a whopping Rs 3,869.5 crore. This include ₹ 3,269.5 crores of broadcast and streaming revenue and ₹ 200 crores and ₹ 400 crores of central sponsorship and title sponsorship revenues, respectively.

After much speculation, at the time of this book going for print, IPL S13 was held from 19 September, 2020 to 10 November 2020 in UAE. The season was played without a live audience in the stadiums. The broadcast happened with "recorded sounds" of "audiences" to boast morale of the players as well as off-sit viewers. While families around the world were watching it on television, the players were allowed to take along their own families as per the Standard Operating Protocol issued by BCCI. The game is ON!

IPL and Allied Benefits for Team Owners

Table 2.2 elaborated the team owners of IPL teams. India Cements, one of the team owner, has been an active participant in the TNCA League Championship, one of the most professionally run championships in the country. India Cement has sponsored 12 Cricket Clubs spread over all the five divisions of the TNCA League and is present at some of the popular Tamil Nadu Cricket tournaments like the Buchi Babu Memorial Trophy instituted in 1910 and the Hindu Trophy which was inaugurated in 1950. The teams sponsored by India Cements have triumphed in the Buchi Babu Tournament three times and have emerged victorious in the Hindu Trophy 11 times. India Cements has been trying to break free from its conservative mold, trying to grow beyond its traditional southern markets. Here, running a successful cricket team captained by Dhoni becomes the calling card when it meets dealers and consumers in the north. The company has offered 1,800 new dealers in Madhya Pradesh, Gujarat and Rajasthan, free tickets for CSKs games, coupled with a pilgrimage to Tirupati. The strategy has paid off, cited India Cements marketing head Rakesh Singh writes T R Vivek (2011). As per the Economic Times report of 2011 the company is now able to utilise every bit of its factories capacity.

T R Vivek (2011) highlights how the franchise model of IPL is a win-win situation for all its promoters. He notes with reference to Mumbai Indian (MI) team that it is a valuable managerial training ground for the family and it also provides Reliance Industries Limited (RIL) a platform to extend its corporate social responsibility (CSR) activities. As noted in the article even India's biggest private company would not mind more visibility. Vivek cites Managing Director of Brand Finance M Unni Krishnan saying that Reliance's integration of social and business dimensions gives MI an existence with a purpose, thereby, creating a healthier sporting ecosystem. CSR activities of RIL through five NGOs Pratham, Ummeed, Akanksha, Teach for India and Nanhi Kali that work in education for underprivileged children provides a unique business proposition to attract and associate with global fan base as M Unni Krishnan been quoted.

T. R. Vivek (2011) cites another case of Royal Challenger Bangalore, where the owner realising that running a franchise based in Bangalore would be impossible without the support of the local Karnataka State Cricket Association (KSCA), the team went on to co-opt its officials. RCB emerged as a professional club with a strong focus on innovation in fan engagement, merchandising and ticketing. Its substantial investments in developing corporate stands to create a world-class sports-viewing experience has resulted in higher gate receipts and higher margins for every ticket sold. The franchise has become an extension of Kingfishers tag line '*The king of good times*'.

Singh (2013) has done an interesting story about how IPL helped local companies to grow national because of IPL association. He gives examples of India Cement, GMR group and Muthoot Finance. He cites how associative network model is helping these companies form the neural networks in the audience brains forming the linkages between different nodes (representing concepts/brands) with arcs connecting the nodes. IPL has succeeded in the stronger linkages of respective brand with the players or teams leading to incremental gains for the team owners.

IPL and Sports Business

In 2008, Sharda Ugra in the story for India today notes that taking example of 99 million people or 76% of the total trackable TV audience of 131 million who watched the IPL over six weeks providing brands, advertisers, sponsors and cricketers eyeballs. The average TV ratings for the first 44 games stood at 4.71, regardless of the below-par production qualities indicating popularity of game and its marriage to money. The trend continued with bigger numbers even in 2020.

T R Vivek (2011) remarks the three Business Lessons from IPL S4:

(1) The franchise business model is quite risk free.

(2) A team can help an owners non-cricketing core business brands.

(3) Chennai and Mumbai team owners' have been the smartest strategists so far.

IPL not only changed the cricket in India, but it changed the way sports, sports league and relationship of money with sports. It also created aspiring cricketers in smaller towns of India who dreamt to make money by playing cricket. Most importantly it created an ecosystem for sports leagues in the country.

It paved way for leagues in non-cricketing sports a reality. Cricket League made common people dream about DREAM TEAMS!!

3

Non-Cricketing Leagues

*[Beginning of Non-Cricketing Leagues * Kabaddi League * Wrestling League * Badminton League * Football League * Table Tennis League * Volleyball League * Upcoming Leagues * Valuation Aspects]*

This chapter elaborates non-cricketing leagues and their connections to Indian sports scene and their standing in international sporting events. Kabaddi, Wrestling, Badminton, Football, Table Tennis, Volleyball and few upcoming sports leagues being in a process of having leagues have been discussed.

Bhanu Pande in his March 2012 Economic Times article remarks that five new professional leagues were announced in the last 18 months and, word is, two others are being revived. Citing Shailendra Singh, joint managing director, Percept India, agency behind the Indian Boxing League (IBL) the article notes, "The Indian sports consumer is looking for entertainment, diversion, passion and emotion...League sport will ensure that." The article further cites CVL Srinivas, chairman of Starcom Media Vest India, a global communication and media services group, stating that while sports is a good medium for brands to connect to the youth, the most popular of them, cricket, poses an entry barrier for many advertisers and many advertisers today see cricket as overpriced. He has been cited saying, "Emerging new leagues could give them an opportunity to enter sports in some way at a much lower cost." Pande further comments that the new leagues learnt from the mistakes of the past and either took the boards of their respective sports along (soccer, boxing and basketball) or worked towards it (hockey).

Beginning of Non-Cricketing Leagues

In a way sports league history in India belongs to other sports and not cricket. Football league started in 1996 which converted to league format in 2007. Premier Hockey League (PHL) was started in 2005 but it closed down within three years as reported by Joy Bhattacharjya (2016) and Bhanu Pande (2012). Though other sports leagues started before cricket, its only cricket league in form of IPL that provided visibility to league formats. Pande (2012) cites the reason for the failure of PHL that the teams were all owned by ESPN and all the matches were held in Chandigarh. He quotes Darshan M, CEO of Machdar Motorsports, promoters of i1Super Car Race Series "IPL has proven that city loyalties exist, which has prepared the ground for other professional sporting leagues to take off."

Table 3.1: Non-cricketing leagues in India

No	*Sport*	*Name of Sport League (Year of inception)*	*Year of First & Last Season*	*Number of Seasons by March 2020*	*Partner Media Channel*
1.	Football	I-League (National Football League-1996)	2007	24 (NFL-11 &I league-13)	Zee Sports, Ten sports, Star Sports
2.	Hockey	Hockey India League (2013) World Series Hockey (2012)	2013 2017	5	Star Sports
3.	Badminton	Premier Badminton League	2013	5	Star Sports
4.	Golf	Golf Premier League	2013(First & Last)	1	Sony Six
5.	Tennis	International Tennis Premier League	2014 2016	3	Star Sports
6.	Football	Indian Super League	2014	6	Star Sports, Hot Star
7.	Kabaddi	Pro Kabaddi League	2014	7	Star Sports
8.	Wrestling	Indian Wrestling League (2013) Pro Wrestling League	2015	4	Sony Pictures Network India
9.	Table Tennis	Ultimate Table Tennis	2017	3	Star Sports, (Online-Hot Star) & Jio TV
10.	Cue Sports (Billiards & Snooker)	Cue Slam, Indian Cue Masters League	2017	1	Sony Pictures Network India

(Contd...)

11.	Tennis	Tennis Premier league	2018	2	-
12.	Volleyball	Pro volleyball league	2019	1	Sony Pictures Network India (Online : Sony LIV)
13.	Boxing	Indian Boxing League (2013) Big Bout Indian Boxing League (Backed by Federation)	2019	1	Star Sports
14.	Basketball	Indian Basket Ball League (2013) UBA Pro Basketball League	2015 2017	4	Not recognized by Basketball Federation of India
15.	Kusti	Zee Maharashtra Kusti Dangal	2018	1	Zee Talkies
16.	Car Racing	I1 Super Car Series (2013) X1 Racing League	2019	1	-
17.	Kho-Kho	Ultimate Kho Kho	Proposed	-	-
18.	Handball	Premier Handball League	Proposed	-	-

Source: Compilation by author based on varied sources.

Table 3.1 elaborates inception of non-cricketing leagues.

Kabaddi League

India has been doing well in indigenous sport (Kabaddi) at the Asian Games and has won seven gold medals out of eight since inclusion of this game in 1990. Kabaddi is played throughout India from the village to district level on soil. As a sport it does not need any sport equipments. The Pro Kabaddi League (PKL) is a professional-level Kabaddi league in India. It was launched in 2014 (https://www.prokabaddi.com/). The website remarks that the Amateur Kabaddi Federation of India (AKFI), participating members of the International Kabaddi Federation (IKF) and the Asian Kabaddi Federation (AKF), support this league.

It started with eight teams and player auctions on May 20, 2014. It is backed by international broadcasting giant STAR India and S1 ran for five weeks. S2 was during July 2015 and S3 was telecast just after five months of completion of S2. In S4 in June 2016, 24 international players from 12 countries also joined the game. S5 has been the longest in the history of the league with 138 matches played over the period of 13 weeks. S5 added four more teams-Gujarat Fortune giants, Haryana Steerlers, Tamil Thalaivas and U.P. Yoddha.

There are 12 teams in Kabaddi league representing all the metro cities of India. The league is played indoors making broadcasting of the event easier in terms of telecast management. As the game is growing, the prize money is also increasing every year reaching one million USD in the Season Six in 2018. As BBC business news reported at the time of its launch in 2014, the game was treated as IPL of Kabaddi because of the association of Indian film stars and cricket celebrities. Initially running cost of each club was around USD$800,000 including salaries and travel. Now, the league has gained the title sponsorship with a Mobile Phone Company and Season Seven was played from July 2019 to October 2019. Due to Pandemic 58 is now shifted to 2021.

Most expensive player for Kabaddi was auctioned at the start of Season Seven at 10.5 million USD and total 441 players participated in the auction for all 12 clubs. Not only Indians but Iranian players also participated in this league season. Star Sports is a paid sports channel for Indian audiences. In 2015, it was decided to have two seasons in same calendar year but post S5 viewership witnessed declined.

The bidding auction for PKL media rights will go for ten-year cycle in 2020. Inside sports desk story of December 2018 cite dissatisfaction amongst team owners about lack of transparency and conflict of interest amongst broadcaster and one of the league owner. Star India as a broadcaster also holds majority stake in Mashal Sports, one of the league owner entity. The article cited one of the team owners saying, "We are confident that the league management will act in a responsible manner to ensure that all stakeholders are able to derive the best value for the league. With the tremendous market for kabaddi in India, TV and Digital rights can unlock significant value for the league and we are hopeful that there will be an open, transparent bidding process, as can be expected from a professional league anywhere in the world."

Wrestling league

Wrestling is a popular sport in rural India. Like kabaddi, wrestling is played not on matt but on the soil in the most part of India. Most of the wrestlers come from the rural or semi urban backgrounds. Pro Wrestling League (PWL) was started in 2015 with six teams. The teams have nine players each with five men and four women. There are five domestic players and four international players in each team. The names of the teams are Bengaluru Yodhas, CDR Punjab Royals, Dilli Veer, Haryana Hammers, Revanta Mumbai Garuda and UP Warriors.

The third season was played in January 2018 for 18 days with 20 Olympic and world champions taking part in the game. In S3, two-time Olympic medalist Sushil Kumar, debuted having been paid Rs 55 lakhs in an auction representing Delhi Sultans. Total six teams participated in the fourth Season held in 2019. Usually the league is played in January.

The League website (http://www.prowrestlingleague.com/) remarks that the League has:

- 51 Olympians (23 Men & 28 Women)
- 20 Rio 2016 Olympic Medalists
- 30 World Championship Medalists
- 13 Continental Games Champions
- 34 World & Continental Champions

The format and style of game is based on Olympics system and wrestlers from Asia, Europe, Africa and America participate in the league. This league has many familiar faces from India like Sushil Kumar, Bajrang Punia, Sakshi Malik who have won the medals at the Olympic and Asian games. League is broadcast on Sony Pictures Network India and Ten sports. According to BARC India data for Week 3 (January 13-19, 2018), PWL was consistent on Sony Wah (Free to Air Channel of Sony Network) and happen to have the best ratings for any ongoing sports league in India.

Badminton League

Badminton League (https://www.pbl-india.com/) is organised by

Badminton Association of India (BAI) and played with round robin and knockout format. BAI was formed in 1934 and has been organizing national tournaments since 1936. The Premier Badminton League (PBL) was launched in 2013 and has so far completed five seasons. The glamour factor of this league is Olympic medalists Saina Nehwal and PV Sindhu. The world top players such as Lee Chong Wei and Carolina Marin also play for this league. The broadcast rights have been bought by Star Sports besides sports broadcasters of US, UK and Hong Kong have also bought the media right for their own territories. The league has franchises from Mumbai, Lucknow, Chennai, Bengaluru, Hyderabad, Pune and Guwahati.

Football League

India has 36 State associations affiliated with All India Football Federation- AIFF (https://www.the-aiff.com/). It is way back in 1872 that Calcutta Football Club was established. The formal federation was formed in 1937 which had no Indian members till 1920s. National Football League (NFL) was founded in 1996 but was re-launched and rebranded in 2007 as the I-League. Saurabh Mishra in his 2015 article notes that NFL came into existence as the idea was to have Pan-Indian participation in a league format in order to promote the sport in a uniform manner. In 2007, the AIFF decided to replace the NFL with the ONGC I-League in an attempt to revitalise the state of football in India. Indian Super League (https://www.indiansuperleague.com/) started association with Star Sports and IMG. Due to change in the title sponsorship it became Hero I-League in October 2014. The website of ISL states that India's leading industrialists and celebrities from sports as well as the Indian film industry have heavily invested in the league's ten franchises based in the following cities: Chennai, Bhubaneshwar, Goa, Guwahati, Kochi, Kolkata, Mumbai, Hyderabad, Bengaluru and Jamshedpur.

In 2010, AIFF had signed a 15 years' agreement with Mumbai based Reliance Industries Ltd. (RIL), and International Management Group (IMG), in a bold move to accelerate the growth of football by revamping the league structure in India. IMG exited the business quietly in 2018 just ahead of its Fifth Season. As per the AIFF agreement, RIL-IMG were granted all commercial rights including sponsorship, advertising, merchandising, broadcasting, film and video data, franchising and new league rights and intellectual property rights, related to football in India. It is broadcast on Star Sports, Hot Star & Jio TV (Digital platforms).

The league runs annually for six-months during October to March. Number of national and International football players associated with Indian Super League (ISL) has managed to get a foothold in football states such as West Bengal and Kerala but fail to have all India presence. There are eleven franchises and has multiple broadcasting partners like Fox, Turner, Brit Asia, Abu Dhabi Media Company, MTEL, Perform/DAZN and Saran to reach the globe.

Table Tennis League

The name of Table Tennis League is Ultimate Table Tennis (UTT-https://www.ultimatetabletennis.in/). There are six teams and top Indian and International table tennis players are participating in the league. Star Sports is the broadcast partner of the league. This league started in 2017 and normally it has two week' schedule for a season. This league is supported by Indian Table Tennis Federation (http://www.ttfi.org/) and the players have performed at the international level and brought laurels for the country. Table tennis players such as Manika Batra and Sharath Kamal won the medals in Commonwealth Games 2018 and Asian Games 2018 who are also associated with the league. The 2020 edition was deferred due to Covid-19 pandemic and it will be played in 2021 as reported in October 2020.

Volleyball League

Pro Volleyball League (PVL- http://www.provolleyball.in/) started in February 2019 as a venture between Baseline Ventures India Pvt. Ltd, Volleyball Federation of India and Title sponsor in form of financial technology company for four Season. The broadcasting partner is Sony Sports network- Sony Six, Sony Ten 3 and Sony Liv online platform. The first season saw six city based teams playing total 18 matches at Chennai and Kochi. The premier Fin-tech debit

Card Company is the title sponsor of the league. The Second Season was played with 22 matches in February 2020.

Kho-Kho League

The indigenous game of Kho Kho is played in around 20 countries, mostly in Asia. India witnessed the launch of Ultimate Kho Kho League (http://ultimatekhokho.com/) in April 2019. It is a joint venture of Kho Kho Federation of India (KKFI- apex body of the sports in India) and Dabur India Ltd. Eight City based teams were to compete with each other and it will be televised too. Interestingly the league website has no further details about seasons scheduled in September 2019. There is Sportskeeda article of December 2019 citing KKFI General Secretary that it will be played in 2020 but pandemic apparently derailed the plans. Kho Kho league is the brand new entrant in franchise based model of sports leagues in India, still to swing into action.

Upcoming Leagues

Athletics League: The participation of Indian athletes has always been highest in numbers at the Olympic, Commonwealth and Asian Games. The Athletics Federation of India (AFI) is the apex body for running and managing athletics in India started in 1946 and is affiliated to the IAAF, AAA and Indian Olympic Association. AFI (AFI- https://indianathletics.in/) as reported in *The Hindu* (2016) has been thinking about athletics leagues on the line of IPL. Especially 100 meters and 200 meters' races in athletics have always been blue ribbon events with global fan base. India has not won a single medal in Athletics in the Olympic games so far, but athletes such as Milkha Singh, PT Usha and Anju Bobby George raised the bar of Indian athletics and upcoming athletes such as Neeraj Chopra, Hima Das and Duttee Chand seems to be determined AFI has as many as 32 affiliated state units and institutional units.

Swimming League: India had won one gold at inaugural Asian games way back in 1951 after that there has not been much progress. Although India has yet to set record has not been very impressive at the international level in swimming but it can be an opportunity for the Swimming Federation (https://swimming.org.in/) to expand the game. United Sports Federation of India started as open water Swimming Competition in 2019 as Swimming Premier League (https://swimmingpremierleague.com/). Interestingly the league website has not a single registration and not much information.

Quiz League: Gaurav Laghate in his June 2020 article about forthcoming Quiz League quotes educationist Protichi Lahiri Sengupta, one of the founders of the 2019 startup which plans to launch franchise-model based professional quiz league - ProQuizzin League. She has been cited saying "The cost of organising this league is also much lower compared to other sporting leagues. Purely from a safety and health point of view, we will get all the teams to one city and shoot indoors." ProQuizzin League plans to extend merchandising opportunities and online gaming. The founders have been organising "one of World's biggest quizzing festivals called the Kolkata Quiz Festival for the last 10 years". Yet it needs to be noted that Quiz is not a recognised sport by Olympics Committee.

League Valuation Aspects

CII-KPMG report, titled 'The Business of Sports - Playing to win as the game unfurls' remarks that during 2013–15, eight major league-based sports tournaments were launched; these include Indian Super League (ISL), Pro Kabaddi League (PKL), Premier Badminton League (PBL) and Hockey India League (HIL). Cricket maintains the stronghold in sports advertising with 51 percent share in on-ground sponsorship, 61 percent in team sponsorship and 64 percent in endorsements. League-based events for other sports, such as football (Indian Super League) and kabaddi (Pro Kabaddi League) have seen on-ground sponsorship in 2015 increased to a noteworthy 300 percent for kabaddi, 91.6 percent in football, 53.5 percent in marathons and 32 percent in tennis. ISL was able to double its central sponsorship pool from the first season in 2014 to the second in 2015 — earning approximately 100 crores. PKL also generated sponsorship revenue of ₹ 45 crores for its broadcaster and investor Star India. PKL is the first most valued non-cricketing league with ₹ 60 crores worth of title sponsorship.

Considering the relationship of sports, society and business with broadcasting, it appears that the sports leagues in India are here to stay and grow multifold. Cultural variables like increasing number of working parents keep their children occupied with the television or mobile on their own and sports provides pass time activity irrespective of gender as proved by IPL seasons viewership data.

Nuclear family with lesser social ties or little interest in meeting relatives may find League match outing more economical and another alternative to going to Cinema Hall!!

4

Organisation and Management of Sports Leagues

*[Sports Education in India * Business of Sports * Sports League Organisation * Economics of Sports Leagues * Media Coverage of Sports Leagues * Media and Sports Leagues * Aspects of Media Management in Leagues * Intersecting Interests]*

The year of 2005 was declared as International Year of Sport and Physical Education (IYSPE, 2005). The United Nations document elaborates role of the sports mainly from following perspectives:

- Sports and physical education as a human right
- Sports as 'school for life'
- Sports, physical education and the Rights of the Child
- Sports as investment in public health
- Sports for individual and community development
- Sports as a tool in conflict transformation
- Sports as a training ground for democracy
- Sports as a tool to promote peace
- Sports for people living with disability
- Sports for a holistic development of a child

When sports leagues are a phenomenon new to India, besides sports persons, there are a whole lot of people who work behind the scene like coaches, fitness trainers, sports nutritionists, ground staff, talent management teams, public relations people and so on to make the sports person deliver his/her game. While many of these people are trained on the job, many self-train themselves over the years and now there are institutes training students for work in this area.

Professional sports need infrastructure in terms of playgrounds, ground management, playing pitch maintenance, sports equipments, sports garments, and technical equipments for play execution and monitoring, equipments for fitness and maintenance and so on. FICCI's Vision document of the year 2014 had estimated human resource requirement of 43.7 lakh people across the sports industry by 2022 in India.

Paul A Staudohar and James A. Mangan in their edited volume on 'professional sports' (1991) divides league sports into three categories; labour (players and unions), management (owners and leagues) and government (those defining public policy and regulator of actions of labour and management- preserve and protect fans and sports event entertainment at the same time follow the rules of the game). In India, little has been written about labour and governance whereas leagues owners and batting associated with the sporting event has stolen the media limelight in the last decade.

It needs to be recognised that formal education in sports and sports management is still at a nascent stage in India. Without trained human resource, talent nurturing and training infrastructure cannot expect world class performances in global sports arenas. Indian sports federations are also under controversies for varied reasons. Formal education in sports may change the scenario in future.

Sports Education in India

In India, the Sports Authority of India (SAI) is an organisation responsible for sports related matters. As the website suggests (https://sportsauthorityofindia.nic.in/), it is a successor organisation of the Sixth Asian Games held in New Delhi in 1982, set up as a Society registered under Societies Act, 1860 by the Department of Sports, Govt. of India. The objective is to promote sports and games and it has the responsibility of maintaining and utilising, on the behalf of Ministry of Youth Affairs & Sports, the following Stadia in Delhi which were constructed/renovated for the Asian Games;

- Jawaharlal Nehru Sports Complex

- Indira Gandhi Sports Complex
- Major Dhyan Chand National Stadium
- Dr. Shyama Prasad Mookherjee Swimming Pool Complex
- Dr. Karni Singh Shooting Ranges

The Society for National Institutes of Physical Education and Sports (SNIPES) consisting of Netaji Subhash National Institute of Sports (NSNIS), academic wing at Patiala and its two branches; Laxmibai National College of Physical Education (LNCPE) Gwalior-Madhya Pradesh (http://www.lnipe.edu.in/wordpress/) and (https://www.lncpe.gov.in/) Thiruvananthapuram-Kerala were merged with SAI *w.e.f.* 1st May 1987. The LNCPE Gwalior was however, delinked from SAI in September 1995 and has become a "Deemed University".

National Sports University, Manipur was established by the act of parliament in 2018 is under Department of Sports, Ministry of Youth Affairs & Sports. This university offers courses such as BSc Sports Coaching and Bachelor of Physical Education & Sports for the undergraduate students besides postgraduate programmes like M. Sc. Sports Coaching and MA Sports psychology.

There are few private institutes and private universities also offering courses in sports management. International Institute of Sports Management, Mumbai (https://www.iismworld.com) offers Bachelor's and Master's degree in Sports Management and Post Graduate programme in sports management and sports event management. National Academy of Sports Management- NASM Mumbai (https://www.nasm.edu.in/), Symbiosis International University (Deemed), Pune offers courses such as MBA in Sports management and *Banasthali Vidyapith* Rajasthan offers specialisation in Sports Management.

Business of Sports

Any Sport has multiple allied businesses associated with it. It is not about a sport per se but an entire ecology of sports person and his/her support networks. A sport also is not played in isolation. It can be individual or team sport. For an individual sport, sports person has to bear expenses in terms of food and nutrition, fitness and diet needs, game practices, sports gears and accessories, coaching and training, infrastructure hiring, sports medicine and sports technology, image maintenance and so on. The sports person earns come from winning the game, brand/corporate/ endorsements, media appearances, government stipends or salaries due to job on sports quota.

In India, the Central and State governments support sports competitions at various levels, funds infrastructure creation and Sports Authority of India get funded by the state for training of sports persons. National Federations and State and District Sports Associations conduct games at block, district, state and regional levels. Infrastructure creation and talent counting and grooming are essential areas for sports development. In India private investment in sports infrastructure is limited through three modes- PPP (Public Private Partnership) model, 'For profit' academies and strategic initiatives and lastly through CSR (Corporate Social Responsibility) and non-profit participation. In February 2016, Government accorded industry status to sports infrastructure reading to increased interest amongst private players.

KPMG (2016) notes four key metrics of success in sports; sponsorship, viewership, broadcasting and performance. The report remarks that cumulatively 635 million Indians watched ICC 2015 World Cup. FIFA World Cup was watched by 55 million Indians where proportion of men and women was 16:11, little difference across gender. Sports especially after IPL has become accepted form of family entertainment as evident from television viewership data.

The Sports teams especially in league business need geographical connect, will have to put up the performance on ground, cultivate fan base, manage and market their affairs and can encash celebrity influence. Sports persons and sports teams are vehicles through which marketers want to reach their audiences. Marketers and advertisers want to reach out to viewers using sporting event telecast; using media; to gain extended reach. Products, people, services, ideas; anything and everything can be sold through media during matches. IPL has number of case studies about product launches and advertising campaigns like Vodafone ZooZoo campaigns (since IPL S2), Havells fans (since IPL S3) and many others. Smartphones, Cellular Phone Services and Internet/Online Shopping categories remain the top three advertised categories during IPL telecast. For celebrities, businessmen and even politicians who want to remain in public memory, sports leagues provide opportunities in the midst of sporting event. League broadcasts can help models, fitness trainers, designers, dieticians, and many others apart from league owners, sports persons, media and advertising agencies, media professionals and so on to reach out to masses.

Sports League Organisation

A league can adopt two types of schedules: a round-robin or an elimination tournament. In a round-robin, the league creates a schedule of games for a championship season and every team plays a predetermined number of games against other team of league members. The champion is determined by aggregating the results of all matches.

Noll and Patel (2003) in their article on Organisation of sports leagues compares operations and outcomes in Europe and North America, and concludes that the European system of promotions and relegation is superior to the closed structure of American leagues, and that the American system of multiple parallel leagues to determine qualifications and seeding in a post-season tournament is efficiency enhancing.

"Sport administration, the way it is run in India, through coteries, cabals, manipulations and intrigues, seems to discourage a vast majority of the population to devote itself to athletics, shooting, judo, table-tennis, gymnastics, soccer, boxing, fencing and the like," wrote Delhi High Court Justices Bhat and Waziri in their May 2014 judgment. Ali in his January 2020 article for Outlook India remarks that ironically, politicians play a crucial role forming rules that govern sports; a conflict-of-interest issue. Still, the National Sports Development Bill, 2013 and the Sports Code for Governance in Sports, 2017 are hanging fire for years, with administrators resisting change and refusing to embrace transparency.

Sports Ecology>>	Infrastructure Development	Governance	Talent Scouting& Training	Sports Marketing
	• Funding • Arenas	• Sports Goods • Manufacturing • Norms & monitoring	• Sports Retails • Coaches & experts	• Sports Events
Stakeholders>>	**Government Bodies**	**Private Entities**	**Public Private Partnerships**	**Autonomous bodies**
	Ministry of Youth Affairs and Sports, Sports Authority of India, Sports Institutes	Sports Goods Exporters, Training Academies, Broadcasters, Advertisers, Advertising Agencies, Sponsors, For Profit Franchises, Event Companies, Private shops and online retail, Monitoring bodies, Spectators		IOA, National Federations, State and District Sports Associations, Valuation Agencies Media

Adopted from KPMG Report, Business of Sports 2016, Pages 10 & 23

Figure 4.1: Organisational Aspects for Sports Leagues.

Economics of Sports Leagues

KPMG Report of 2016 defines eight stakeholders in sports ecology in India; Funding, Sports Marketing, Infrastructure development, Governance, Talent scouting and training, Sports goods manufacturing, Sports events and Sports retail as shown in Figure 4.1. Each aspect of these stakeholders needs to make money for the league to survive and thrive as a business and need to be entertaining for audiences. David Turney (2017) in his paper on valuation of sports leagues remark that the "Buyers of sports franchises are typically wealthy individuals for whom the attraction of ownership is based on its perceived "ego" or "trophy" value, as other individuals might purchase a new sports car.

There are five types of sponsorships- on ground, team, franchise fees, sports persons/endorsements and on air. Large part of sponsorship comes from on air, in other words broadcasting income. With digital media the broadcasting rights have gone further from radio in older times to television to now internet and mobile content distribution rights. While the broadcaster buys 'broadcasting rights' from the league management or league promoters, they recover it through sponsorship income.

KPMG (2016) report notes that Indian sports sponsorship market increased from ₹ 40.3 Crore in 2010 to ₹ 61.9 Crore in 2015. The franchise (Companies or individuals owning teams) enter into the business of the game through league management/promoters. Apart from maintaining their own teams, they make money through sponsorships, merchandising and keeping their players and team brands active across media platforms. KPMG Report further remark that franchises are not making profits and eight ISL franchises estimated to have lost close to 35 to 40 crore in its first season. In case of PKL, the overall investment is normally around ₹ 14-15 crore per season for each team. This is partly covered by broadcast fees of around ₹ 6.5 crores per team. However, this still leaves losses of several crores per season. This is the main reason why the broadcasting of the PKL is in doubt for its 2020 season.

It is evident from the nature of league ownership (Table 4.2 and Table 4.3) that the most people involved in the league business are having their own business interests in multiple other businesses. As elaborated at length in the chapter on IPL League, how a Cement manufacturer due to his involvement with BCCI can expand his Cement market by owning a cricket team and the largest Indian Corporate can showcase its social interest through its league team.

Turney (2017) in his paper remarks that the major expense in the league business is that of player acquisition/purchase expense. He explains that "a revenue model has been set for each league and it expands according to the popularity of the sports. There are two key factors which are important for the leagues, Revenue and expenditure." Table 4.1 explains the revenue and expenditure for each of the participants associated with the league process- League owners, franchise owners, Broadcasters and sports persons.

Table 4.1: Revenue and Expenditure in League Business

	Revenue	***Expenditure***
Sports League Promoters	National & Global Broadcasting rights (TV, Digital & Radio), Ticket Sales, Central Sponsorship (Title & Associate League Sponsors)	Ground hires charges, Advertising and Promotions, Federation Fees

(Contd...)

Franchisee Owners	Sports persons/endorsements, Merchandising, Monetizing Fan base, Team Sponsorships (Kits, T Shirts, Badges etc.), Franchise owned Sports Academies in the Cities.	Player Acquisition, Sports Equipment, Team Practice expenses, Training/ Coaching/ Maintaining Teams, Franchisee fees
Broadcasters	Advertising, Subscription, Downloads	Broadcasting Rights, Technology and People for Covering and Telecasting of the sport
Sports Persons	Playing Fees	Self-Maintenance

Source: Compiled by Author.

Bhanu Pande (2012) has explained case of Premier Soccer League (PSL) launched in 2012 in West Bengal. He notes that the Uro Infra Realty, a Kolkata-based real estate company which was the highest bidder for a franchise – ₹ 25 crores for Team Barasat over 10 years, or a franchisee fee of ₹ 2.5 crore per year. Each team can spend up to ₹ 12.5 crore on players, which means Barasat (Uno Infra) will spend a total of ₹ 15 crores a year. Half of the central revenues - essentially, the sale of TV rights and central sponsorships – get equally divided among the six franchisees. In return, each team gets ₹ 2.5 crore as match rights fee for its five home matches. Then, each team can have eight sponsors, apart from ticketing and hospitality rights in home matches. Pande cites Bhaswar Goswami, executive director, CMG, the promoter of PSL "considering the league will be broadcast in 50 countries other than India, it won't be a problem for franchisees to recover their investment."

Franchisor, usually associations, allow franchisee (team owners) to use the brand name of league and manage their own teams at the Payment of fees.

Table 4.2: League ownerships by Business Houses

No.	*League*	*Owners or Corporate Group*
1.	Cricket League (Also see Table 2.2)	Reliance Industries limited, Diageo through United Spirits Limited, Sun TV Network, Chennai Super Kings Cricket Ltd, GMR & JSW Sports (Jindal South West Sports), Red Chillies Entertainment & Mehta Group, Mohit Burman, Ness Wadia, Preity Zinta, Karan Paul, 8. Amisha Hathiramani (Tresco International Ltd), Manoj Badale (Emerging Media (IPL) Ltd), Lachlan Murdoch (Blue Water Estate Ltd), Shane Warne

(Contd...)

2.	Badminton league	R. Sivakumar, Aditya Meesala, Matrix Teamwork Badminton Pvt. Ltd, Slash21 Sports Management Pvt. Ltd. Sahara Adventure Sports Ltd. The Eastern Warriors Pvt. Ltd, Agile Entertainment Pvt. Ltd., Bombay Badminton Private Limited, Tapsee Pannu& KRI Talent
3.	Wrestling League	Olive Sports Pvt. Ltd. (Dipin Kapur, Goldie Behl, Himanshu Khanna, Bhupender Singh, Neeraj Jalan), Revanta Group, Pradeep Sherawat, Anurag Batra (Chairman of BW Businessworld), Katiyal brothers (Honey Katiyal and Sunny Katiyal- Investors Clinic), Dharampal Rathi & Bobby Deol
4.	Kabaddi league	Future Group (Kishore Biyani), Kosmik Global Media, DO IT Sports Management India pvt. Ltd. (Radha Kapoor), Adani Wilmar Ltd (Goutam Adani), JSW sports Group (Parth Jindal), Abhishek Bachhan, KVS Energy and Sports Limited (Rajesh V Shah), Insurket Sports pvt Ltd.(Kailash Kandpal), Blasters sports Pvt Ltd (N.Prasad, Sachin Tendulkar), Veera Sports (Mr. Srinivas Sreeramaneni of Vaya Group, Mr. Goutham Reddy Nedurmalli of NED Group and Mr. Mahesh Kolli of Greenko Group), Unilazer Ventures Pvt. Ltd (Ronnie Screwvala), GMR Group
5.	Volleyball League	Bonhomie Sports Event Mgmt. Ltd, Agile Entertainment Pvt. Ltd. Beacon Sports, Thomas Muthoot, Chennai Spartans Pvt. Ltd, U Sports (Ronnie Screwvala)
6.	Boxing league	Adani Group, Aditya Goyal, Sanjive Narain, Deepak, Colonel Dev Negi, Dilip Pandey, SportzLive & Prospotify
7.	Football League	RPSG Group (Dr. Sanjiv Goenka, chairman of the RPSG Group), ATK Mohun Bagan Private Limited, Sourav Ganguly, Utsav Parekh, JSW Group (Jindal South West), Vita Dani, Abhishek Bachchan, Mahendra Singh Dhoni, Goan Football Club Pvt. Ltd. (Jaydev Mody, Akshay Tandon, Virat Kohli), Vijay Madduri and Varun Tripuraneni, Rana Daggubati, TATA Steel, Blasters Sports Pvt Ltd.(Chiranjeevi and Akkineni Nagarjuna, Allu Arvind, Nimmagadda Prasad), City Football Group (65%), Ranbir Kapoor & Bimal Parekh (35%), John Abraham (Film Actor), GMC Group
11.	Table Tennis League	U Sports (Ronnie Screwvala), Aishwaryaa, Rajinikanth, Dhanush and Sameer Bharat Ram, Mr. Shrinivas Dempo, (chairman of Dempo Group from Goa) Mr. Vivek Bhargava, DoIT Sports (Radha Kapoor Khanna), InsureKot Sports Pvt (Mr. Suresh Kotak), Sanjiv Goenka, chairman of RP-SG group and Utsav Parekh.

Source: Compiled by Author.

KPMG 2016 report titled '*The Business of Sports: Playing to Win as the Game unfurls*' provides detailed economics of league business and remarks that the revenues earned by the major global leagues overshadow any league in India, including IPL. The report highlights 'cricket betting' as another industry associated with cricket leagues. Party discussed in second chapter.

Table 4.3 shows names of celebrities and their association with the sports leagues investments. Considering that for media celebrities, having league ownership proves win-win situation because when leagues get broadcast on television or digital media, it provides visibility to the celebrity for free. Also their visibility quotient helps to get advertisers for the respective league teams.

Table 4.3: Relationship of Leagues and Celebrities

No.	*Name of Celebrities*	*Sports leagues*
1.	Shahrukh Khan	Cricket
2.	Preity Zinta	Cricket
3.	Virat Kohli	Football
4.	Hrithik Roshan	Football
5.	John Abraham	Football, Hockey
6.	Sachin Tendulkar	Football
7.	Abhishek Bachchan	Kabaddi, Football
8.	Ranbir Kapoor	Football
9.	Shilpa Shetty	Cricket
10.	Juhi Chawla	Cricket
11.	Late Sushant Singh Rajput	Boxing
12.	MS Dhoni	Football
13.	Sourav Ganguly	Football
14.	Randeep Hooda, Sohail Khan, Suniel Shetty, Riteish Deshmukh and Rana Daggubati	Boxing
15.	Tapsee Pannu	Badminton

Source: Compiled by Author.

Media Coverage of Sports League

In any sports league match broadly three types of personnel: media, ground and team staff are involved. In order to understand the position of technology and people, example of the Cricket and the Football ground with camera positions have been illustrated in the Figure 4.2 and Figure 4.3. In any regular Cricket league match broadcast, there are usually 12 cameras placed.

As shown in Figure 4.2:

Camera 1 shows the Batsman who is facing the ball and **Camera 2** remains with the ball. Both the cameras are placed at a certain height so that they can cover the whole ground along with the player.

Camera 3 & 4 repeats the same action in same way, when the batting side is changed.

Camera 5 is placed at height at mid-wicket position and it covers the whole ground and both the batmen ends with a side view.

Camera 6 & 7 covers the slips that are the diagonal ends of the ground and are placed at the ground level to cover the catches at the slips.

Camera 8 & 9 shows the slips view, when the right handed or left handed batsman comes on strike. Both the cameras are at the ground level.

Camera 10 and 11 remain at a height of Cam 1 to 4. These two cameras follow and capture the ball closely; tracing the swing and spin of the ball. These are called Super Slow Motion Cameras.

Camera 12 is a hand-held camera that follows the batsman when the enter or exit the ground and at times it is placed at ground level and is moving camera.

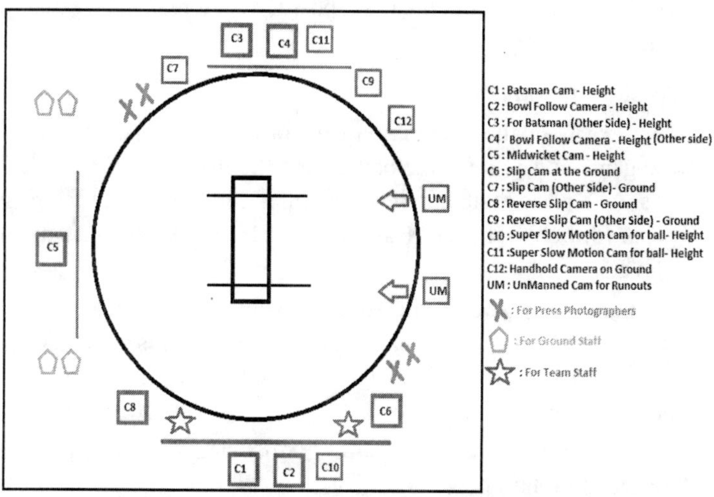

Figure 4.2: Cricket Ground Camera and Personnel Positions.

Two unmanned cameras are also kept on ground to cover the crease on both the sides and to capture run-outs. Press Photographers are placed at the ground level outside the boundary rope. Ground staff is positioned outside the boundary rope and they are supposed to take care of pitch conditions and cover the ground in case of rains. In order to make them reach the pitch quickly they are always in the ground, placed near the boundary. During the T20 matches, players are placed in the Dugouts which are outside the boundary rope and team and support staff is also positioned in the dugouts only. During the One-day international match and Test matches, team and support staff are provided the team rooms on both the sides of the ground.

Figure 4.2 clearly indicate the amount of administration and management required in order to cover the ongoing match. Chapter 5 discusses technological options being incorporated to capture minutest details of players' expression and sounds for the viewers sitting in the comforts of their homes getting first-hand 'live' experience of being on the ground.

Figure 4.3 illustrates football match ground with camera and personnel positions. In any conventional football match broadcast, there are at least eight cameras on the location. FIFA world cup final match get covered by more than 50 cameras and most of them are unmanned (automatic) but the basic positioning remains the same as illustrated in Figure 4.3.

As shown in Figure 4.3:

Camera 1 is called the master camera which covers the 70% of the game and follows the ball during the match. Camera 1 & 2 positioned at certain height so that they can cover both the goal posts while ball moved. **Camera 2** is placed for the close up of players.

Camera 3 is placed at the ground level to take the reactions of the players. In every football match all the cameras are placed at one side of the ground for the continuity and screen direction providing ease to the viewers.

Camera 4 & 5 are for tracking the off side and they are also placed at certain height.

Camera 6 & 7 are for the tracking the goal post and are placed behind the goal post.

Camera 8 is handheld camera for the reaction of the coaches and team members who are sitting in the dugouts outside of the ground. Dugouts are at the side lines of the ground for coach and extra members of the both the sides. Press Photographers are allowed in the ground but outside the periphery of the ground. They are placed behind the goal post on either sides during football matches.

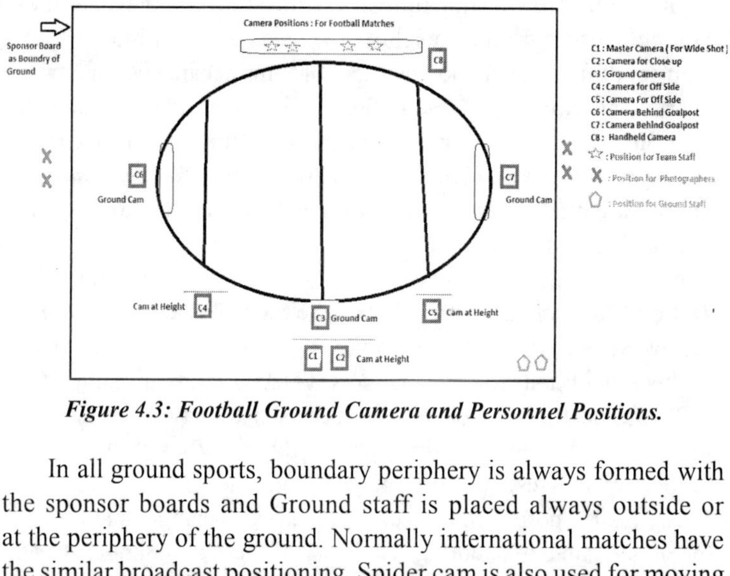

Figure 4.3: Football Ground Camera and Personnel Positions.

In all ground sports, boundary periphery is always formed with the sponsor boards and Ground staff is placed always outside or at the periphery of the ground. Normally international matches have the similar broadcast positioning. Spider cam is also used for moving Ariel shots that covers ground and galleries in order to capture audience reactions for the audience sitting at the sports venue. In league business, sportspersons team kits which include Jersey, trousers, Helmet, Clothes, kits also become places for advertising with logo of sponsors. There is also merchandising of these jerseys as fans want to cheer for their favourite team by the way of wearing their favourite team, jerseys.

As sports persons too are required to be part of the show business due to their association with brands and sponsors makes it inevitable to have them remain in public memory. India has many sports persons married to film actresses!

Media and Sports Leagues

Media plays a very important role in sports league business. Franchises owning the teams need 'on ground' performance, sponsorships, marketing, team management, celebrity influence whereby visibility and fan engagement. While here only Hindi films have been elaborated, in India Sport is a subject of films across languages.

Relationship of film industry with sports league has been symbiotic. Apart from ownership of leagues by celebrities, sports is a subject of films. Post 2000, number of films became popular taking a particular sport as a subject. Set in 1893 pre-independent India, 2001 film '*Lagaan*' was Oscar nomination featuring game of Cricket. Hockey became part of Hindi film in 2007 with '*Chak De! India*'. In 2013 '*Bhag Milkha Bhag*' was a biographical Hindi feature film on Indian athlete Milkha Singh, national champion and Olympian, also known as flying Sikh. The year 2016 witnessed two Hindi films- '*Dangal*' and 'Sultan' both based on the sport of wrestling. '*Dangal*' was based on the struggles of women wrestlers- Geeta Phogat (Gold) and her sister Babita (Silver); winners at Delhi Commonwealth Games in 2010, and their father as well as coach Mahavir Singh Phogat brought the sport into the limelight. Bollywood flick 'Sultan' about fictional male wrestler also promoted the game. Film like *Saandh ki Aankh* in 2019 portrayed lives of sisters-in-law Chandro and Prakashi Tomar and game of shooting. The story of these two Shooter Daadis of Uttar Pradesh's Johri village is also a story of empowerment in otherwise patriarchal and discriminatory rural milieu. In 2020, the film 'Panga' was released on the theme of woman Kabaddi player from urban India.

While Indian media give lot more importance to the game of cricket and cricketers, in last two decades' other sports too are gaining eyeballs. On August 19, 2016 Olympics badminton final, in which PV Sindhu won her silver medal, had 66.5 million viewers tuned in, the highest viewership India received by a single match, according to data sourced from Bengaluru-based media-tech start-up, ZAPR reported by The Economic Times. Many non-cricketing athletes are now gaining corporate contracts, media coverage and recognition.

Hotstar runs a show on its channel titled "Kabaddi ke Crorepati" (https://www.hotstar.com/in/tv/kabaddi-ke-crorepati-2018-hindi) in multiple languages. 'Son of Soils' on Amazon Prime tells the story of a Kabaddi team from Jaipur. The story modelled on the lines of BARCA FC league takes viewers inside the dressing room and group dynamics and players as well as owners' pressures to win the game. 'Cricket Fever-Mumbai Indian' ran on Netflix, 'Roar of the Lions-Chennai Super Kings' on Hot Star are IPL programming content garnering fan base as well as creating audiences through OTT.

Aspects of Media Management in Leagues

Since league matches are broadcast, media is the integral part of showcasing of sporting expertise as well as game spirit. ICC Cricket World Cup of 2019 played total 48 matches across 11 different venues and these were to be live streamed. Carter (2019) notes that London-based Sunset+Vine, global production partner of the ICC, used a mobile broadcast unit, five technical teams, four production teams, 24 commentators, and 32 cameras to cover each match. That included drones, super slow-mo, eight ultra-motion Hawk-Eye cameras, Buggy Cams, front and reverse view Stump Cams and Spidercam. A 15-second graphic countdown clock to DRS was shown on screen and in the ground. The technical aspects have been elaborated in the next chapter but it needs to be recognised that the human, technical, intellectual and economic resources need to work in synergy for broadcasting or streaming of each match, series of matches and number of seasons.

Media and leagues are married to each other and sponsors and audiences away from the ground provide the support for sustaining the relationship of the league business. While it is important for the players to remain in public memory, media acts as a vehicle to make them 'popular' and desirable. Their popularity get them brand endorsement as well as visibility to their teams as well as team owners. At the same time the same visibility can put them in trouble as well. In 2018/19 two Indian Cricketers made certain remarks on a Television chat show which did not go well with the Committee of BCCI Administrators and disciplinary action was taken against both of them.

Media works as double edged sword for league business. Media helps in reputation management of all the players, league owners, sports persons, teams, sponsors, service providers of the teams and so on. At the same time, media can spoil the reputation of the same people either for vested interests or for the misconduct by any of them. There are number of examples in the Indian context as one elaborated above.

Shergold Adam (2020) remarked that 300 to 500 people are needed for Premier League Football closed door match due to the Pandemic. Imagine for a game involving only 40 players need paraphilia of 32 coaches and medical staff for two teams, 12 match officials, six to eight doctors and medical personnel, three premier league officials and 130 or more media personnel. Club directors, security, stewards, ground staff and scoreboard operators have yet to be counted. Match officials comprise of a total of six plus six Hawk-Eye staff to operate the goal-line technology, the communication systems between referees and their assistants, and the Video Assistant Referee technology besides four people responsible for doping control and another four to move the 'matchday furniture' including signs branded with sponsors seen before kick-off. This shows the nature of administration and management required for league matches.

Intersecting Interests

Sports leagues began as local event but with transnational television made its presence global. Leagues come into existence for a particular sport, after their inception and decisions about format and broadcast tie-ups, the money behind the leagues as investment has to ensure Return Of Investment (ROI) so gets added glamour, expansion plans, the Players auctions and brand tie-ups to promote leagues to ensure viewership. As elaborated in IPL chapter, any sports league provides social, political benefits for the team owners besides their economic investment. It provides them with visibility and presence whereas performance is very challenging to retain.

It needs to be recognised that in order to retain novelty, sports matches cannot be played every day. League usually runs for 30 to 45 days in a year but sponsors want to have visibility 365 days a year. In order to keep the league property alive, allied activities are required. League owners and franchises have to think about keep it a long term sustainable business. That is possible only if league is part of other interests of owners as well as sponsors. Many sports persons also invest into league business since they understand their profession. Media being integral part of league business keeps people associated with the league in news for some reason or the other. Figure 4.4 illustrates stakeholders in league business.

Gaurav Laghate (2020) in his report for Economic Times cites the seventh edition of an Annual Report "Sporting Nation in the making" by ESP Properties; the entertainment and sports Division of

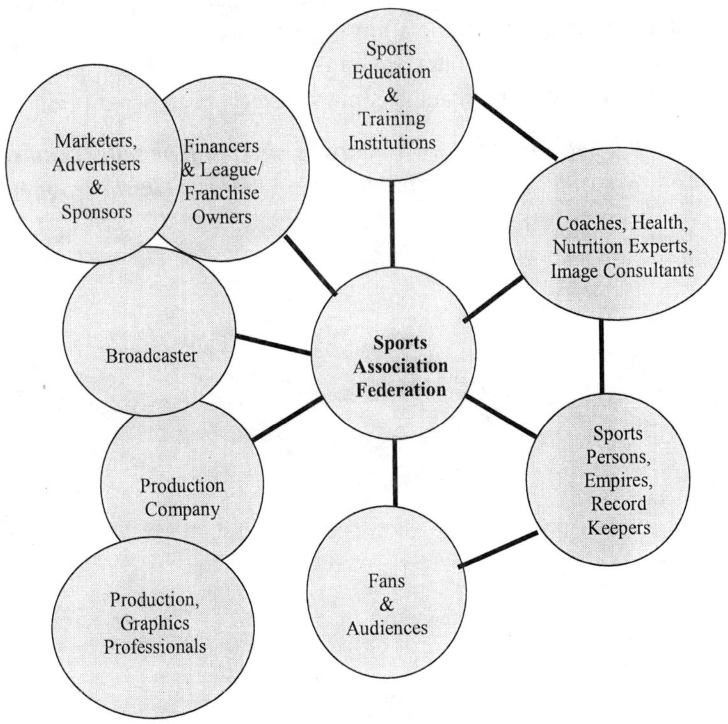

Figure 4.4: Stakeholders in Sports League Business.

Group M India and notes that the overall sports sponsorship in India has grown 17% in 2019 to cross ₹ 9,000 crore mark. As per the report, the on-ground sponsorships have grown by 25 percent and media spent by18 percent whereas the spent on digital media shot up whooping 84 percent. Social Samosa in its 25 September 2020 story about "A Consolidated list of IPL Brand Collaborations 2020" remarks that there have been new kinds of sponsors due to pandemic besides the older ones in form of "hygiene partnership and official mask partnerships", added to the conventional merchandising. Figure 2.2 shows the type of sectors associated with IPL 2019 teams."

The only purpose of league business is to make money and sports become secondary to the exhibition of sporting competence. Many players have been cited saying that T20 is not the real cricket yet they play it because it gives them fame and money. Brands want to reach the audiences, audiences want entertainment and sports persons want fan base so the association of everyone involved in league business is nothing but intersection of their own interests. Leagues are going to stay in the years to come for everyone to benefit from it.

As it is said- so far there are buyers, there will be sellers and so the market. Since there are viewers and so there will be the leagues!

5

Broadcasting and Sports Leagues Relationship

*[Global Broadcasting Spectrum * Players 'off the Ground' * Broadcasting Technology in Sports * Sports Channels in India]*

Sports have become an accepted form of entertainment now. Since radio was invented before television, audio broadcasting of sporting events was recognised in earlier times but that reality changed after the arrival of television. In early years when sports were mainly supported by the government, matches and sporting events used to be telecast on television. With the privatisation and satellite television, sporting events became global and games have audiences beyond geography. Sports can be recorded or live depending upon technological and economic implications of the said event. Sports leagues are designed on the lines of live events in India clearly making them entertainment than sports!

With digital technology, it has become possible to undertake live sports broadcasting. It is directly associated with the viewership and revenue. Broadcasting of any sporting event would have stakeholders in terms of broadcasters themselves who make money by selling air time, advertisers (who can sale their products and services to viewers), sports persons (who can exhibit their performance and also create brand of themselves), commentators (who get paid for their work and also get recognition), technicians (who have their livelihood doing telecast) and obviously audiences who are curious to be part of the game on the ground or off the ground. The off the ground audiences are not only in their homes but also can be in bars and restaurants since that is another form of entertainment being promoted in urban India.

Global Broadcasting Spectrum

Over the last couple of decades, the sale of broadcast tune, and particularly television rights for sporting events and competitions has become an extremely profitable activity, giving birth to a global industry worth about US $30 billion (PricewaterhouseCoopers, 2011). The Indian Media Entertainment Industry Report of 2016 notes that the amount of investment by Star Sports is 200 billion, Sony Six invested 193 billion, Ten Sports to the tune of 6 billion and Neo Sports 120 million in their operations in US dollars.

The International Telecommunication Union (ITU- https://www.itu.int/) is the United Nations specialised agency for information and communication technologies – ICTs. It was founded in 1865 to facilitate international connectivity in communications networks Covering fixed and mobile radio services, satellite systems, radio and TV broadcasting, radio navigation, meteorological monitoring, space research and Earth exploration, as well as amateur radio. Live sporting events use satellite spectrum and globally different satellite footprints are used for the live telecast. Table 5.1 shows an example of Hero ISL Footprint globally which is covered by different broadcasters and Indian diaspora across the global must be watching it from their respective homes. With digitisation and Internet people can search for their respective sport league coverage and connect on Over The Top (OTT) channels or Video On Demand (VOD) provided by streaming companies. With reference to IPL 2020 Season, News18 cited Cricket Bet India's research about 11 percent rise in IPL viewership in the UK this year whereas reduction in EPL (England Premier League) which 'might have relations to the newly introduced Pay Per View system'.

Since 2015 broadcasters took interest in the broadcasting rights of international sporting events for Indian audiences. SPN (Sony

Pictures Networks) through Sony Six was exclusive broadcasters for *La Linga*, Spanish football league and NFL Super Bowl for Indian viewers. Star India acquired rights for German football league Bundesliga in 2015 and has rights to air Formula One events in India till 2022. It also aired Rio Olympics across its channels to India, Pakistan, Bangladesh, Bhutan, Maldives, Nepal and Sri Lanka.

Table 5.1: Example of Hero ISL Footprint

Territory	*Broadcaster*
MENA*	Abu Dhabi Media Company
Sub-Saharan Africa	Fox
Australia	Fox
Brazil	Turner
Bulgaria	MTEL
Germany/Austria/Switzerland	Perform/DAZN
Turkey	Saran
UK & Ireland	Brit Asia

Source: https://www.indiansuperleague.com/news/hero-isl-s-global-footprint accessed on September 10, 2020.

[***MENA** countries consist of 19 countries namely, Algeria, Bahrain, Egypt, Iran, Iraq, Israel, Jordan, Kuwait, Lebanon, Libya, Morocco, Oman, Palestine, Qatar, Saudi Arabia, Syria, Tunisia, United Arab Emirates and Yemen].

Table 5.1 shows how Hero ISL is received in 19 countries indicating global viewership for this football league due to network broadcasters' agreements. The broadcasting rights are usually auctioned by the league owners to the broadcasters. For example, Star India's broadcasting rights deal was a game changer that made IPL at par with the global sports properties on a fee per match basis. https://khelnow.com/ has done a story on November 18, 2020 stating that the future of Pro Kabaddi League (PKL) broadcasting is in trouble due to disputes between broadcaster and team owners. The report notes that the Star Sports thought to have offered a 14-15 crore per season share from the media rights to each team against team expectations of 22 crores per season leading to delays. Since the broadcasting rights were originally up for renewal for the 2020 season, but its cancellation means that the new agreement will now cover the next five seasons, starting next year. The delay in decisions, further hampered due to Covid-19 pandemic, may create disappointments for Kabaddi fans.

Players 'Off the Ground'

Star India's broadcasting rights deal enhanced their network value. While any sports get played on the ground, there are number of players "off ground" that makes the league become popular and profitable. Broadcasters are the first people who connect the game with the audiences but there are production companies, sporting technology vendors, entertainment companies, advertising agencies, broadcast graphics vendors, team owners and sports persons, sports regulatory authorities and many others who make sports league viewership enjoyable for the off-site audiences. Broadcasters make money either by subscription or by advertising.

Shuchi Bansal has done an opinion piece asking a question "Will Star India benefit from IPL media rights deal? On September 7, 2017 for Mint. She notes that Star India agreed to pay to the Board of Control for Cricket in India (BCCI) ₹ 16,347.5 crore for five years for the global media rights—both digital and television—for the 10-year-old Twenty20 cricket tournament. Two months ago, Chinese handset maker Vivo Electronics Corp. had paid ₹ 2,199 crores for five years to BCCI to be the title sponsor of the property. Before Vivo, PepsiCo Inc. had agreed to pay close to ₹ 400 crore for 5 years although the deal was terminated in 2015. Sponsors, league owners and broadcasters are main players in sports broadcasting.

Bansal (2017) provides the data of media industry estimates stating IPL made ₹ 1,300 crores in ad revenue for Sony in 2017 of which ₹ 400 crore a year from distribution because of IPL. The network also increased the Advertising rates. In 2016, Sony Pictures Networks (SPN) introduced separate IPL inventory sales for standard definition and high definition channels. For IPL 2017, SPN reportedly quoted spot rates of over ₹ 6 lakh for SD channels and ₹ 2 lakh for HD feed. The distribution rights for digital streaming and worldwide distribution also provides revenue to the broadcasters.

Shefali Bindiya (2020) has done a story for indsidesports on IPL 2020 and she states that putting both Regional and Hindi+English sports channels together a total of 145 brands were advertised in IPL 13 with Dream11.com being the title sponsor. This is an indictor enough for number of players for one leading sports league so imagine all leagues and broadcaster put together the volume of business. There are companies like Kadamba (https://www.kadamba.com/) from Chennai or Deltatre (https://www.deltatre.com/sport) globally that makes sporting broadcast experience enjoyable by making it as their business. Such technology companies are others players in the league business.

Broadcasting Technology in Sports

In order to reduce the costs, automation is an important aspect of the broadcasting. Robots are taking over the reins of technology and men or women in the front or behind the camera are being replaced by robots. The critical challenge for the sports broadcasters is updating of technology to bring the newest experience for the audiences. Such technology advancements are demanding, expensive and would need resources not only in terms of money but also human and managerial expertise to keep pace with the technology. The increased cost of the technology will have to be borne by none other than the viewers.

The four main aspects of sports broadcasting are: Visuals, Sound, Game analysis and its presentation through graphics and animation. Digital technology for recording, replay and broadcast has been changing the way sporting events are being shown to the off-site viewers. With Artificial Intelligence and Augmented Reality becoming part of broadcasting sector, sporting events have become real-life experience in the drawing rooms of the television viewer.

While in the olden days' cricket was about technique and commentary, today it's about telecast and streaming. Jamie Carter has done a story about new technologies at ICC World Cup 2019 listing following technological innovations in cricket, most of which earlier were used in football and other global sports already.

- **STATSports Trakers:** Indian National Cricket Team signed-up with UK sports technology company STATSports, for wearable performance-monitoring tech, essentially a fitness tracker built into a base-layer vest that's loaded with sensors that measure distance, speed, acceleration, deceleration, high-speed running, and the dynamic stress load of each player.

- **Piero graphics analysis system:** It's a 3D graphic where several camera feeds along with CricViz (https://www.cricviz.com/) and score predictor can be used together at a click of a button.
- **Spidercam:** The shots aerial sweeps and angles, formed the environment for pop-up AR (Augmented Reality) graphics of key players, and even the trophy itself get virtually placed in the middle of the ground.
- **360 Degree Replays:** Multiple camera feeds to be stitched together to create wrap around video, 360-degree video replays of matches were made available online on ICC TV.
- **BatCams; BatcamFLY and BatcamDRIVE:** BatcamFLY is a drone equipped with a 360-degree camera that can produce an eye-line shot before racing up to 400 ft for an atmospheric overview/skyline shot. A remote-controlled 10x zoom camera on wheels also has GPS tracking. Batcam DRIVE are remote-controlled 10 × zoom camera on wheels that travel at up to 30 mph having GPS tracking. These are used for replay shots from behind the wicket-keeper.
- **TRACAB Optical Player Tracking:** It shows viewers the exact field position of players as well as a range of data points, including running speed and distances covered.
- **Hawk Eye:** LBW detection- Six cameras, three at each end of the ground, Hawk-Eye essentially tracks the ball and predicts its path. Ultra Edge- Stump microphones that clearly differentiate between the sounds created by different sources, specifically the bat, pads and clothing of the batsman.
- **Hotspot:** A tracking system that constitutes two SLX-Hawk infrared cameras that measures heat from friction to produce a frame showing the precise points of contact of the ball which was part of DRS- Decision Review System.

The Website dedicated to Sports + Science elaborates (https://www.topendsports.com/sport/cricket/technology.htm) technologies associated with cricket. Following is brief description of these technologies under four broad headings - Visuals, Sounds, analysis and graphics. In Kabaddi league, the matt is used to show team mascots and animation for the on-site as well as off-site audiences.

(i) Visuals: Visuals are the most important aspects of the live sporting events broadcast on television or digital platforms. Visuals with cameras, graphics and motion capture makes the viewing experience as real as possible for the audiences sitting away from the venue. It makes them feel that they are on the ground.

- **BALL TRACKING:** First came into showing the path of the cricket ball way back in 2001, now it has become the most used part of the Decision Review System (DRS) for adjudicating LBW decisions. Apart from ball tracking, it offers analytical data, magnification, speed of the bat swing, release points for bowlers. It is used in tennis, soccer and many other sports. It uses six or more computers linked television cameras around the field and produce accurate 3D trajectory of the ball and sends it to VR machine. There are brands like Hawkeye, Virtual eye etc.
- **HOT SPOT:** This technology usually used for review if ball touched the bat, glove or pad, using two infra-red cameras positioned at either end of the ground. If there is contact of ball with the bat, cameras sense and measure heat from the friction generated by a collision.
- **LED WICKET (STUMPS & BAILS):** In July 2013, ICC approved use of flashing stumps and bails called wicket in cricket and was used for the first time in ICC World T20 of 2014. When the bat, gloves or ball hits the bails or they get dislodged from its groove, the stumps and the bails start flashing red usually. This Australian technology uses low voltage batteries in the bail when loses contact with the stump gets illuminated making wooden stumps and bails thing of the past. This also made the third umpire's work easy and provides clear visuals for the television audiences.

- **STUMP CAM & MIC:** The Stump camera and microphone creates a sense of being physically present on the pitch for a viewer and also provides an ear to interesting banter or mind games that go on between the batsmen, bowler or close-in fielders. Stamp camera also helps in determining catching decisions.
- **CAMERA IN THE UMPIRE'S HAT:** Another innovative experiment was done during the production of Indian Premier League (IPL), by placing a camera in the umpire's hat providing a different kind of viewing experience.
- **SPIDER CAM:** These camera provides Ariel view or bird's eye view enabling the film and television cameras to move both vertically and horizontally over a predetermined area, typically the playing field of a sporting event such as a cricket pitch, football field or a tennis court. It is called Spider cam because it is attached with 8 strings and is always in the air so that viewers can see the team meeting and can also experience different angles of the players during the game.
- **BUGGY CAMERA:** The presence of the BUGGY CAMERA gives a tracking shot at the ground level and it runs in the ground in a straight direction or around the boundary line in a circular direction.
- **ULTRA MOTION CAMERAS :** These cameras are able to record moving pictures at an astounding 1000 frames per second, giving the chance to see moments in slow motion.
- **TOUCH SCREEN:** Another technology commonly used these days in studio by the presenters is screen filled with data being touched by the presenter and showed while talking. As the name suggests, video clips showing match analysis are presented with a touch of a finger by the presenter.
- **HELMET CAM:** Weighting less than 100 grams including camera and batteries, helmet camera for batsmen were first introduced in 2012. IPL seasons used them extensively for the viewers to get the feel of the ball speed and providing first person batsman angle. It also helps in run out decisions.

(ii) Sound: Digitisation has brought about smaller and sleeker devices in terms of size and convenience of handling sound devices. Interviews, mics at the ground, sound made by players, audience response to the game; all of these have become possible with microphones installed at multiple locations on and off the ground. Earlier even if visual was captured, the sound reality was never so accurate. IPL 2020 used recorded audience sounds due to absence of live audiences, creating new trend because of Pandemic.

- **SNICK-O-METER:** This is a very sensitive microphone embedded in one of the stumps and connected to an oscilloscope displaying sound waves. This meter picks up the sound when the ball hits the bat showing the trace in slow motion video for television audiences.
- **FIELD TALKBACK:** Microphones are given to fielders/ players on ground who can chat with commentators or directly with the television audiences. In live matches usually the fielders who are on the boundary are engaged using such microphones for making the audiences part of the game.
- **COMMENTATORS:** Since its inception commentary are the most integral part of sound in sporting events. With the advancement of technologies, audiences are part of narrative discussion with commentators and commentators also have 'face' to themselves.

(iii) Analysis: AR (Augmented Reality) Graphics, Touch-Screen and Virtual Reality gives the 'real' viewing experience and understanding to the audiences on and off the ground. The game of sports has gone into sea change where strategies, predictions and analysis of opponents' game are as much part of playing as rest of the things. Data and management of performance, planning and reviewing, team management using strategizing and coaching are essential aspects of any sport today be it league or galli sport.

- **SPEED GUN** – Speed guns or radar guns are used to measure speed using radio wave technology. The gun has radio transmitter and receiver. The Ball Revs tracker as the name suggest calculate the extent of spin depending on revs imparted.

- **VRS (Video Replay System):** Virtual Reality and 360 degree cameras get used in basketball, cricket, rugby and football. Sensors in the balls and in boundary rope are used to determine boundary decisions. Umpires require feedback for a front-foot or no ball decision for which lasers are installed in the form of a beeping sound if the bowler crosses the popping crease.

(iv) Graphics: Virtual reality sets and 3D graphics have completely changed the way sports broadcast was 10-15 years ago. Graphics have become more informative and automated. Amongst the AR and VR, AR is used in the studio analysis and VR is used for on the ground production. The different graphics such as Wagon Wheels, Pitch Maps, Beehives, Deviation of Seam/Spin, Fireworks, Field Placement, Six Distances etc. can be shown in AR during studio presentations. There are companies specialising in sports graphics even in multiple languages. IPL S3 used 3D technologies during cricket matches and special 3D spectacles were provided to watch those matches.

- **AUGMENTED REALITY GRAPHICS:** This includes the pre and post event analysis of the game. These graphic based 3D pictures can create artificial playgrounds and cut-outs of star players and coaches in the studio with figures and analysis. 3D graphics production and analytical system for sports broadcasters like Piero or Viz Libero uses image recognition and state-of-art graphic outlays which are integrated with the existing production to create engaging visuals to retain broadcast audiences.
- **Goal Detection System:** In Football this radio-based system is used for low-frequency magnetic fields to determine whether or not the whole ball has passed over the goal line. Two magnetic fields: one in the goal area, and the other created in and around the ball processes the data and transmits wirelessly to the referee's wristwatch in real time.

Sports Channels in India

There are 900+ private satellite television channels in India which have been given permission by the Ministry of Information & Broadcasting to broadcast and as per the developments of October 2020 the OTT (Over The Top) as well as digital news sites content have also come in the purview of the Ministry.

Out of the total 902 television channels in 2019, there are 28 dedicated sports channels available for the viewers. Among them, 18 are Simple Definition, and 10 High Definition. Interestingly all the sports channels in India are subsidiaries of global media conglomerates. Two major ones are STAR and Sony.

STAR Group of Channels: Formally ESPN Star Sports, Star Sports is owned by Star India which is a subsidiary of Disney India which is an Asia Pacific subsidiary of American media and entertainment conglomerate Walt Disney, California. STAR as Satellite Television for Asian Region has multiple channels which now speaks multiple Indian languages.

The Company website (https://www.startv.com/about-us/sports/) notes that there are 17 channels with premier sporting events in the purview of ICC, BCCI and leagues like Indian Premier League (IPL) New Zealand Cricket Board, Bangladesh Cricket Board and Asian Cricket Council (ACC); Tamil Nadu Premier League (TNPL); Karnataka Premier League (KPL); Caribbean Premier League (CPL); VIVO Pro Kabaddi, Football under Hero Indian Super League (ISL) Hero I-League; Hero Super Cup; Premier League; Bundesliga; Badminton under Badminton World Federation (BWF) events; Premier Badminton League (PBL); Ultimate Table Tennis (UTT); and other sports such as Formula 1, Wimbledon, The French Open and US Open. STAR has channels now telecasting in Hindi, Tamil, Kannada, Telugu, Bangla, and Marathi.

Sports broadcasting have also become local with Sony Six, new sports channel of SPN which telecast games in Tamil and Telugu languages. ICC World Cup 2015 was the first event telecast in six languages- Tamil (Vijay TV), Kannada (Suvarna Plus), Malayalam (Asianet Movies), Bengali (Star Jalsa), Hindi and English. Pro Kabaddi League is telecast by Star in five languages over eight channels. IPL in 2018 was telecast in six Indian languages besides

Hindi and English. Language broadcasting helps regional advertisers to reach their audiences through sporting broadcasts while making money for the broadcaster. The Hindu Business line, 17 February 2015 reports that the advertising spot of ten seconds were sold at ₹ 50,000 to ₹ 1,25,000 even in regional broadcasting. Sponsorships and advertisers are essential for sustenance of the respective sport.

Figure 5.1: STAR Group of Sports Channels beamed in India.

SONY Group of Channels: Sony Pictures Network India Limited (https://www.sonypicturessportsnetwork.com/) has group of eight channels as shown in Figure 5.2. Each of these are dedicated to different sport for example Sony Six is for Cricket and NBA whereas

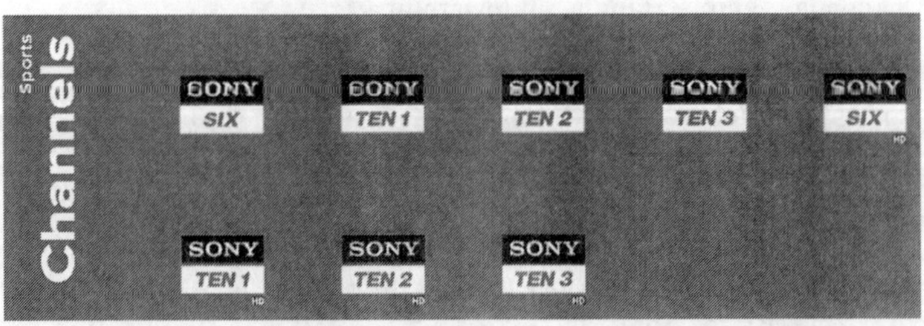

Figure 5.2: SONY Group of Sports Channels beamed in India.

Sony TEN1 for WWE, Sony TEN2 for Football, Sony TEN3 for marque sporting properties even with Hindi commentary.

Other sports channels in Indian subcontinent are Eurosport, Eurosport HD (Earlier known as Dsport & Dsport HD) and DD Sports (Public service broadcaster). From the total 28 channels, 19 sports channels are in English language, 4 sports channels are dedicated to Hindi language and 5 channels belong to regional languages; Tamil, Telugu, Kannada, Bangla and Marathi.

Apart from television broadcast, mobile and broadband subscriptions are the game changers for sports consumption. As per International Telecommunication Union data in 2011 out of 100 inhabitants 0.94 people had mobile-broadband subscriptions which has become 49.37 in 2019. This refers to "individualised" consumption as people are watching sports on their mobile devices or computer screens and other handheld devices. Fantasy sports is another dimension of leagues. Dream 11 as title sponsor of IPL 2020 season made it possible for the viewers to make their own virtual teams. Across sports fantasy gaming is another emerging area due to VI and AR technologies. It's the excitement of winning and pain of losing that makes sports viewership emotional journey yet the mechanised devices create the viewing, an experience!

Technology increasingly is replacing human resource but at the end of it, viewers will have to be human for the leagues to make money!

6

'Common' Across Leagues

*[Template of League Business * League Presence in Broadcast Space * Patronage & Support from National Federations * Association of Bollywood & Cricket Celebrities * Ownership by Business Houses * Length of the League & prize money * The Revenue Model * Issues of Governance * The Gender Angle]*

Every sport league in India has got a common thread- money, power, passion and competence. This chapter sheds light on those similarities which can be labeled as DNA of the sports leagues. The ultimate goal of any league is to make the leagues financially viable so that they can be sustained. The game has to remain entertaining and engaging for its audiences and fans at the same time generate revenues too. Many leagues; cricketing or non-cricketing, started and closed down because they could not be financially sustained. After the financial success of Indian Premier League, most league owners are focusing on sustaining it for long term and attempts are being made for generating alternate revenue streams and building fan base on and off the sporting grounds.

Template of league business

All the sports leagues in India are City based. This league model has remained successful, tried and tested even for the start of the future leagues. League presence in broadcast space, fan base due to celebrities, presence of film stars, promotion of merchandising, appearances in TV shows are some of the activities taken up by league owners and players. The revenue model is already set for the future leagues as Broadcast rights may be the money puller of the new arrivals. Apart from it, franchisel owners can have the sponsors on the Team Jerseys and Gate money also goes to the Franchisee owners. Each of have the leagues team named after the city as it is done in English Premier League, National Basketball Association and Spanish football league. Bhanu Pande (2012) notes that other sports leagues follow the IPL model, which is city-based and essentially pays for itself by riding on a big TV rights sale. He cites Yannick Colaco, chief operating officer of Nimbus Sports, "any successful league the world over has had two fundamental elements: multiple ownership and multiple match locations." And these locations create diverse audiences on the ground, in order to create local fan base and also novelty for offsite audiences.

League presence in Broadcast space

Roger Noll (2007) has an interesting discussion paper on Broadcasting and Team Sports at Stanford University. He notes that television rights are the largest source of revenue for league in rich countries. He remarks that this growth of revenue from television has gone to half or more, only in the last ten to fifteen years especially in West. Initially league owners were skeptical about television broadcast rights because the fears were that it would impact ground attendance but subsequently it was recognised as additional, rather main, revenue opportunity. Today broadcast Experience on Sports Channel is must for each and every league to sustain and grow fan base also. The revenues generated from broadcast rights ultimately affect the overall revenue model of the league because the broadcast rights have got the maximum percentage in the pie of total revenues.

Since media rights bring the biggest pie of the revenue for the sports leagues, every league makes sure that it is televised and the programming of the television is always entertaining for getting more eye balls for the television channel, sponsor, sports persons, branding agencies and so on. Broadcasting of any sport event is the biggest platform of connecting and engaging the fans. Apart from broadcast platform, now online rights have become crucial to generate revenues.

Saumya Tewari (2020) in her report of March 2020 informs that the sports rights are expected to touch US $1.3 billion dollars by 2024 in India. In 2019, sports media rights market (across 11 Asia Pacific markets) was 1.1 billion dollars which grew by 5.5 billion dollars compared to previous year. The broadcast rights of Indian cricket league were sold in 2.55 billion dollars (16,347.50 crore Indian Rupees) for the time period of five years starting 2017. In comparison to other famous sporting leagues around the world this amount is little. The broadcast rights of established sports leagues such as football league of England were sold in 13.4 billion dollars for a period of 3 years, broadcast rights of National Football league of USA was sold in 39.6 billion Dollars for 10 years and broadcast rights of National Basketball League in 24 billion dollars for nine years.

In order to provide global comparable about viewership, The Apollo 11 Moon landing was watched live globally by an estimated 650 million people on 20 July 1969 constituting around one-fifth of total population of the world of that time. Another event in 1997, the funeral of Princess Diana was watched by an estimated 2 billion people. In terms of sports, 2012 London Olympics was watched by 3.6 billion people. The 2015 Cricket World Cup was watched by estimated 2.2 billion. In terms of television ratings, The Season 3 of IPL 2010 had Television Rating of 5.6 which became 8.92 in 2012 and in 2013 it went down to 6.9. To provide a context the reality show Big Boss Season had TRP of 11.3 with average of 8.3 on regular TRP in 2020.

Table 2.3 (In chapter - 2) elaborates the growth of viewership of IPL, the longest running league as far as India is concerned. The data clearly suggests how more and more viewers till 2012 watched IPL and subsequently has the digital media viewership. The cumulative number of people who tuned in to watch the first six games in 2012 was 90.1 million, down from 101.77 million in 2011, according to TAM Sports, a division of TAM Media Research, a leading television ratings agency in India. At the same time as per BARC data, the 2017 IPL Season10 had 22.5 percent rise in viewership compared to previous season, making total of 1.25 billion impressions.

Ahluwalia (2017) reports that maximum viewership of IPL came from Maharashtra and Goa, followed by Andhra Pradesh and Telangana. IPL garnered 568 million impressions from the rural areas which accounted for 45% of the total viewership of the tournament. IPL 2018 attracted 202 million viewers on Star India's digital video streaming platform Hot Star, 51% surge over 2017 reach of 33 million viewers. The year 2018 also saw 769 million fan base being reached by IPL covering 567 million through television and 202 million through Hot Star platform. In 2019, Hot Star recorded a reach of over 300 million viewers, with a peak concurrency of 18.6 million viewers for the final match between Mumbai Indians and Chennai Super Kings.

BARC Newsletter of 2018 issue-4 titled "IPL over the years" remark that IPL 2018 garnered 23.7 mn Impressions from Out Of House viewing of live matches across three cities, leading to an incremental viewership of 8 percent over viewership from TV currency panel. This clearly indicates growing market for *sportstainment* on digital platforms amongst Indian audiences. Even for the inaugural season of Pro Kabaddi League in 2014, 435 million viewers tuned in whereas 439 million viewers watched ISL of football. This number was comparable to IPL viewership in the same year to the tune of 552 million as per KPMG (2016) report. Considering such volume of viewers, the matter of broadcasting rights and money receved from it become very

What is critical is the supply of sports rights from the perspective of both teams and leagues, including the consequences of centralising the sale of rights in leagues. Noll (2007) has pointed out that centralisation of sports rights sales does not improve competitive balance or benefit financially weak teams. Digital telecommunications are making television competitive and because of it, centralisation of sales is going to change. The term central sponsorship is very important because about 20 % of the money gained in the central sponsorship pool goes towards organising the competition while the rest is divided among the teams (franchisee). Central sponsorship includes the title sponsor and associate sponsors of the league. He has pointed out that different leagues around the world has adopted different policies and practices for sale of broadcast rights and distribution of revenues from the rights fees amongst members.

Patronage and Support from National Federations

There is a well-defined structure of all the sports federation in the country. Federations are recognised by Ministry of Youth Affairs and Sports. Each and every sport league is officially supported by the respective sports leading body or federation such as Indian Cricket Board, Badminton Federation, Wresting Federation etc. It provides great help in flourishing the leagues and consolidation of all the regional groups. Federation decides the rules and schedule of the league which helps in organising the national championship of the sports. It also provides a mark of certification that no other recognised league comes up in the same sport in the country.

Earlier in 2007, in Cricket when a competitive league started before the launch of Indian Premier League (IPL) which was not supported by India's Cricket Board, it had to pack their bags. The related operations were stopped by the national cricket board, the BCCI. As the Sports federations are the major stake holder of most sports leagues, in return, the federations get the revenue sharing from the franchisees in the form of Federation Fees.

Till the year 2019 there were 56 recognised national sports federations of 56 different sports disciplines, out of these 56 sports federations, 36 are Olympic sports federations which are also a part of Indian Olympic association including summer and winter games. Indian Olympic association represents the country in International Olympic committee, Olympic Council of Asia and commonwealth games federation and Association of National Olympic Committees. The Indian Olympic Association is recognised by the Ministry of Youth Affairs and Sports, Government of India in the same way as the respective sports federation.

Association of Bollywood and Cricket Celebrities

The association of film stars with the sporting leagues such as Cricket, Kabaddi, Hockey and Football helps these leagues in financial growth.

In the same manner, these celebrities can associate with the new leagues and can bring with them not only the required financial support but the support of their followers on social media too. It is another factor which brings glamour to the sport and attracts the fan following. Non cricketing sports also get the visibility because of the association of the film stars and business people. Discussion and Table 4.3 (Chapter - 4) listed celebrity associations with leagues.

Ownership by Business Houses

Big business houses and industrialists are becoming the team owners of sports leagues. It brings required amount of money for the league, help the business houses protect and expand their other interests, maintains the confidence of their stakeholders and attracts more cash for the league. It also helps in bringing more and more sponsors for the teams and helping the league in sustaining the business. Table 2.2 (Chapter - 2) elaborates IPL owners (which are major business houses) and how they are benefiting out of their association with IPL directly or indirectly. Table 4.2 (Chapter - 4) suggests how business houses have stakes across league properties.

Length of Leagues & Prize Money

Every league is set in such a manner that it completes in a week or two except for the IPL. The time duration is decided in such a way to accommodate the window of the international sports calendar. Whenever there is a mega sporting event in the world such as World Cup, Olympic Games, Asian Games and Commonwealth Games, the league calendars are adjusted. Only cricket league runs for five weeks because it is played in the summer season in India when young have vacation breaks from schools and colleges. The year of 2020 is exceptional considering the Pandemic. The length of all the world championships is always scheduled for 10 to 14 days.

The prize money is another aspect which attracts the sporting talent from all over the India and world. Leagues are no more national affairs. With transnational broadcasting and presence of international sporting talent, leagues are global celebration of the respective sport. In order to promote the national talent, there is a restriction on number of foreign players in the respective leagues. Apart from prize money, player auctions and individual valuations are also the attraction for the sporting talent since s/he wants to showcase their sporting expertise besides earning money for themselves.

Table 6.1: Prize Winner Amounts Across Leagues

No.	*Sports League*	*Total Prize money (in ₹ Cr.)*	*Winner Amount (in ₹ Cr. Unless specified)*	
			Winner	*Runners Up*
1.	Cricket	50	20	12.5
2.	Table Tennis	3	1	50 Lacs
3.	Badminton	6	3	-
4.	Wrestling	3	1.9	1.1
5.	Kabaddi	8	3	1.8
6.	Boxing	3	-	-
7.	Football	15	8	4
8.	Hockey	5.40	2.5	1.5

Source: Compiled by Author.

Table 6.1 lists the prize money associated with various leagues. Around the world, football receives the highest prize money across different leagues and championships. In the year 2019, the UEFA Champions League had the highest prize money pool of ₹ 9,100 crores or 1.3 billion U.S. dollars. Formula one race had the prize money of ₹ 5500 crores and the FIFA World Cup prize money was ₹ 4000 crores. Interestingly those losing the game also makes money so in a way its win-win for all the parties except for the owners, if they can not manage breakevens they may choose to sale or close the team.

The Revenue Model

David Turney (2017) elaborates in his paper on 'professional sports franchise valuation' that media revenue and gate receipts comprise a majority of total revenue with sponsorship, merchandise, and other making up across the leagues. Operating expenses for the major sports leagues are dominated by player salary expense, which can vary greatly from season to season and have a large impact on profitability (or lack thereof). The primary sources of media revenue are national and local television contracts, with national and local radio, league-owned sports networks, and digital media also providing media revenue. He is citing gate receipts figures from Forbes magazine for MLB topping with 2.7 billion dollars followed by NFL with 2.2 and NBA and NHL having gate receipts of 1.6 billion dollars each in 2017. He is of the opinion that alternative media companies, mainly digital companies are now obtaining non-exclusive rights for live professional sports leading to increasing fees by technology companies or expanded rights in future.

Noll (2007) points how Sports rights are interestingly not depending upon margin of the cost of production of sports programming versus sports rights. He highlights that it would be uninteresting if the revenues and production costs of sports programmes and of marginal entertainment programming were roughly the same. Sports rights are interesting because they can differ substantially from marginal entertainment programming in the gap between revenues and production costs. Broadcasters can make money if the cost of production is reduced and money raised through advertising is increased.

Another aspect of broadcasting revenue is through subscription. Globally 90 percent of sports channels have subscription model where people pay for what they watch and remaining ten percent is through advertising. In India the situation is opposite where advertising revenue accounts for almost 60 percent of the revenue for the broadcaster. Broadcast fees are also the key source of revenue for the teams in the League. KPMG (2016) reports that half of the revenue of IPL team come from Broadcast fees and Central sponsorship income from BCCI.

Star India and Sony Pictures are investing heavily into comprehensive sports portfolios. Discovery Networks Asia-Pacific (Eurosport) is another player in sports broadcasting market in India. Laghate (2017a) notes with reference to five years broadcasting rights bid won by Star India for IPL that the value of TV rights went up three times and digital by over eight times directly impacting higher advertising rates. In 2017, Star India increased ad rates on TV to ₹ 15-17 lakh per 10 seconds from ₹ 5.75 lakh at the time of writing the article by Laghate while on digital; it took at least three times to

₹ 2.5-3 per impression. BARC Newsletter 2018 issue- 4 notes that during 2016 to 2018, the total number of advertised brands has grown from 138 to 247 (a growth of 79%). The 247 brands that were advertised on IPL 2018 were accounted for by 123 advertisers (count of which has grown 50% since 2016). More and more advertisers are using sports broadcasting, to reach out to consumers.

According to an Economic Times report by Laghate (2017b) the template of running a Badminton franchisee; the total cost (approx. figures) is around ₹ 6.5 crore per year. The three main sources of revenues are central sponsorships, team sponsorships and broadcast rights which are around ₹ 3.5-4.5 crore. More than half of the revenue depends on these three factors. Another source of revenue is from ticket sales or gate money which is approximately ₹ 20 lakhs. This report pointed out about the loss per year which is ₹ 2-2.5 crore and the expected breakeven for the team owner is around five years. This clearly suggest team owners with deep pockets can only survive in league business.

Issues of Governance

Vasavda and Singh (2020) in their Indian Express story of June 26, 2020 notes that in an unprecedented development Sports Ministry derecognised 54 National Federations brining in governance and other issues. Each federation is granted recognition in the month of January which was delayed due to Covid-19. Granting recognition to sports federations is an annual ritual that makes them eligible for government funds as well as assistance for training and competition. Indian Golf Union, School Games Federations of India and Rowing Federation of India have lost their recognition due to governance issues.

Corona Pandemic, as reported by Neeru Bhatia in her article of August 16, 2020, refers to new challenge for anti-corruption officers. Apart from cricket, football and e-Sports held "match fixing" and "pop-up matches" with the intention of corruption and fixing. There are incidences where internet was used to stream a live match and betting was done for the teams. These are illegal processes which get monitored by the anti-corruption unit of BCCI, Investigations- Anti-Corruption Unit of ICC and Integrity services like Sportradar.

Neeru Bhatia (2020) cites Tom Mace, Director of Global Operations Integrity services whose job is to spot unusual activity in betting market or fixing attempts and data fraud. Tom Mace states that they support more than 80 sporting federations and 20 different sports using sophisticated software called the Fraud Detection System (FDS). The article report that there are 600 betting operators globally some are regulated and some are unregulated. Tom Mace has been cited saying that in India the estimated betting turnover decreased by over 60 percent during March and May 2020 due to the pandemic yet the India-facing betting exchange is still generating turnover in excess of Euro 25 million on matches being played in this period.

The Gender Angle

Women sporting leagues and women teams across sports is an emerging area. Women as players as well as women as audiences in Indian context has now been slowly picking up for urban as well as rural India. Number of films around sports themes have also contributed to this increasing visibility of sports not only for livelihood but also as a profession and passion.

All the leagues have tried to tap all types of audiences. In Indian format of leagues, now men and women sports have started to flourish, making it a multiplier for expansion of the sports leagues. Cricket, Football and Hockey has yet to start women leagues while Badminton, Table Tennis, Tennis, Kabaddi and Wrestling leagues have got the mixed teams and women Kabaddi league has already started.

Television viewership of IPL has led to increase in women fan base for cricket in last few years. Number of organisations working for community development has taken up cause of sports for change and sporting opportunities for disadvantaged sections of the society. Talent spotting and training of grassroots sports personnel has been taken overs seriously by sports federations and people are also taking sports seriously considering it as livelihood option. Sports leagues have provided career opportunities for multiple professions and occupations. The 2019 NFL Racial and Gender Report Card issued by The Institute for Diversity and Ethics in Sport (TIDES) at The University of Central Florida stated that racial hiring in the NFL is the worst it has been in the last 15 years. In India, the role of caste, class and religion in sports is an area still to be explored for research and action.

The programming about league players coming from humble background and promotion of their progress on OTT and other platforms is providing role modeling to others. League business is not only changing the sport (Kabaddi from mud to matt and Cricket from Test Match to T20) but also changing the society by creating aspirations and selling dreams. It's creating audiences for stories of hope and courage, competition and perseverance.

India may become next sporting nation if sporting leagues do bigger business since livelihood through sports is now a new reality!

7

The Future of Sports League Business

*[Disruption through technology * Rise of Traditional Games * Impact of Corona Crisis on League Business * Influence on Olympics Performance * Sports Audiences & Society * Way Ahead]*

More than one billion population and India has only won 28 medals at the Olympic Games so far! It is said that performance at the highest level will be as good as the preparation at the grassroots level. Domestic sports leagues are those spaces which provide the opportunity, finances and platform to showcase the raw talent of every serious sports person of the country. That's why the structure of the domestic sports leagues prepares the ground to win an Olympic medal.

Disruption through Technology

Technology has been the biggest disruptor in all the sectors of human lives. Sports leagues will not be untouched with the technological advancements. Apart from technological progress which is making it possible to broadcast league matches on individual mobile phones, Olympic medals have become reality because of sports leagues as witnessed at Rio Olympic in 2016. Figure 6.1 suggest that fan or viewer engagement technologies will be the biggest impact technologies in the coming year, followed by Athlete Performance technology.

Mobile gaming and Esports are two categories which provides futuristic prospects due to the surge of mobile phones and video games

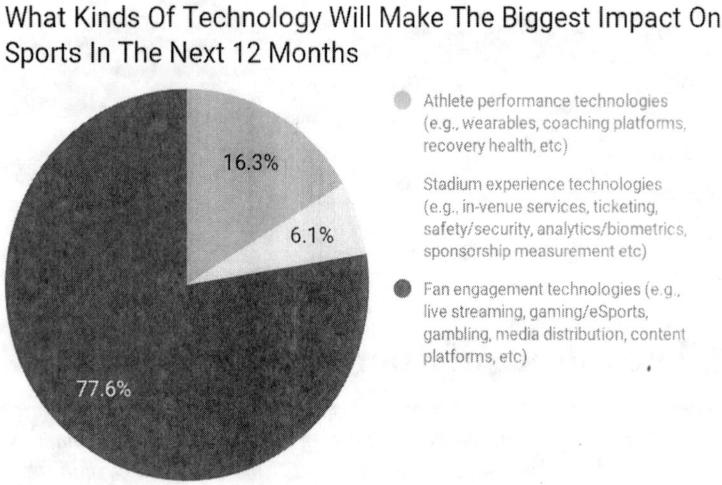

Source: Promon, 2019- https://techcrunch.com

Figure 6.1: Future of Sports Technology.

in India with easy access and available free time, the young users are becoming skilled and experts in playing these games. Esports or e-sport or electronic sports is an emerging area of virtual gaming. In December 2019, Southeast Asian Games played in Philippines. Saw the first Esports competition as medal event sanctioned by IOC (International Olympic Committee). These games were played on personal computers, console and mobiles Esports are unlike video gaming, competitive Chuman-to-human) amateur or professional gaming having spectator element to it. It can be individual or group sport like traditional sports.

The revenues through Esports are expected to reach ₹ 1188 crores (as per the KPMG-IFSG, 2019 report). FICCI KPMG survey report of 2020 also suggests the incremental growth of Esports and mobile gaming in India. Report suggests that the time spent on mobile gaming is increasing and women users are also showing interest. As these young online gaming users will grow in numbers, they will be more professional and it will be a convenient platform to start the online gaming league. Revenues are also coming from the digital platform only as the spending on the digital platform has increased from ₹ 875 crores which is on 84 percent increase from the last year, 2019. Not only mobile gaming, spectators are using mobile platforms because of affordable data rates and surge in users of smart phones. As internet and Smartphones are becoming available, Indian Esports League will soon become reality.

Rise of Traditional Games

After the success stories of Kabaddi and Wrestling and upcoming Kho-Kho league, it's now an established that indigenous games are watched and liked by Indian audiences and players from the villages and small towns can be benefited from such sports. Following are possible future leagues in indigenous sports.

A. **Chess League:** It is said that chess was invented in India and is being played for centuries. India has produced more than 64 Grandmasters so far and it stands fifth in the world after Russia, USA, Ukraine and Germany, when compared in total number of grandmasters in the respective countries. It means chess talents have been strength for India and there is a scope to start the chess league may be in the form of Online Gaming.

B. **Snake Boat Race League:** Kerala has been the destination for the snake boat race popularly known as Vallam Kalli. These races are being played since 1952 in Kerala and each boat has 64 or 128 paddlers to drive the boats. Thousands of people watch the race on the backwaters of God's own country. It is the game of strength, discipline, coordinated efforts. Few of the sports channels have been broadcasting the race apart from the government owned channels. In 2019, the IPL inspired franchisee league model was also adopted and it was named as Champions boat league.

C. **Shooting League:** Abhinav Bindra, Rajyavardhan Singh Rathore, Vijay Kumar, and Gagan Narang are the household names in India as these shooters have won Gold, Silver and Bronze medals in the Olympic Games. India has many Shooting stars and may see shooting league in future.

D. **Archery League:** From Limba Ram to Dipika Kumari, India has produced world class archers who brought laurels for the country. Not only individual events but the team games have the scope to start an Archery league. From the times of Rama and Arjuna, Indian archers are known for their skills, talents and expertise. Private sector such as Tata Archery Academy has already produced world class archers in India. The league may be proved to be another stepping stone for the sport.

E. **Water Sports:** Kayaking and Canoeing sports have been in India for a while and it has the scope for the televised content due to racing, thrill and timing factors. This sport has the national federation and every year national senior and junior championship plet organised. The franchisee inspired league model may do good for the sport.

The League Factor

A. **Financial Support:** The business model or the franchisee model of the existing leagues will become the template for the future leagues and the revenue models will be experimented for the betterment of the sport. The business tycoons bring the sponsors with them and more people associate with the franchisee. The city based sporting franchisee funds the players, coaches and support staff who in turn are funded by different sponsors. Broadcasting Provides sponsors and Franchisee the viewers and fans who in turn sustain the team and league.

B. **Length and City based Location of Leagues:** Most of the leagues are not more than two weeks except Cricket or football leagues because of the scale. Apart from these two games all the sports leagues, Olympic games, Asian Games and Commonwealth Games are always scheduled for not more than two weeks. Shorter leagues can sustain interest.

C. **Support from National Federation:** All the existing sports leagues have received the support of national federations in organising the league. Federations provide necessary support for the players, coaches, referees and others in running successful functioning of the leagues besides sorting out the format and conduct of the matches during the season.

D. **Participation of Reputed International sports persons:** International professional sports persons are part of Indian sports leagues bringing their expertise, fame, fan following, skills and experience in the game. This also helps the domestic players in improving their skill set and exponential growth of the game through sports leagues.

E. **Performance at International Sporting Events:** Commencement of a domestic league is the first step towards an Olympic medal. Leagues help in harnessing local talent and provide them opportunity to play with international players helping them improve their games. Besides leagues also led to increased interest in sports and help promote sporting culture amongst the youth besides promoting non-cricketing sports.

F. **Social Impact:** Leagues are bringing interesting intersection of economic classes and geographies. It is leading to 'national' yet 'local' identity cultivation. Children are aspiring to become sport persons and role models of rural India becoming urban icons because of sports leagues.

Impact of Corona Crisis on Leagues Business

Insidesports.com note that besides the absence of LIVE content, anxiety about the global pandemic affected the sports audience numbers and people turned to news and analysis of updates on the virus spread and its effects. They share that Star Sports may benefit for being the ICC broadcast partner as the world governing body for cricket has opened its archives to television partners for filling the slots created because of the cancellation of the LIVE games.

The future scenario of sports will be impacted in huge way because of the Corona pandemic crisis. Post Corona world will be having many new ways and head scratching has already been started to find ways to organize the sports events in absence of sports fans. In that scenario the Television and online broadcasts will be the main source of viewing as the sports fans will be away from the stadium. It will certainly impact the gate money in the coming days. The dressing rooms will not be crowded and the mode of celebration in the team games will be individual and not in the crowded manner. The following impact can be seen in the future:

(a) International E-Shooting, E-Cycling and Online Chess events have been started in last week of April 2020
(b) Fan less stadiums across the world
(c) No Celebrations and hand shaking for the 'team' games keeping the physical distancing
(d) Precautions during 'Contact sports' where there is a possibility of exchange of sweat and blood.

Corona Crisis will surely impact the financial cost of the domestic leagues. As uncertainty looms while this book. Went for print future of leagues as well as financial position of the athletes too getting impacted. Few studies suggest that Indian premier league has got the valuation of more than 6 billion dollars but the other domestic leagues which have started in last two or three years will have greater negative impact. The revenue model and business cycle of the leagues has just settled and it was on the taking off curve but because of Corona crisis the new revenue models have to be evolved. It will also have impact on the prize money of the league, the match fees given to all the referees, umpires and match officials. It will also affect the bid money for each player too because of the sluggishness in the economy and paying capacity of the sponsors.

Mega sporting events such as Tokyo Olympic Games 2020, Euro 2020, FIFA U17 Women's Football World Cup 2020 and World Athletics Championship 2021 have already been postponed because of Corona crisis. Domestic sporting events and leagues in India has been postponed. There are ten sporting leagues which are organised every year in India which includes: Cricket, Football, Kabaddi, Table Tennis, Tennis, Wrestling, Badminton, Volleyball, and Boxing and proposed Kho-Kho League. The Corona crisis will surely impact all these leagues and people and machine associated with it. It will not only affect the local Indian players but the foreign players too. The logistics, operations, scheduling everything has been rescheduled except for IPL 2021.

Economic Times Brand Equity feature dated August 31, 2020 cites Lokesh Kataria, head marketing, Mattel, saying that the three things that have impacted sports businesses and especially marketers due to Corona are people's changed perspective towards healthy living, being eco-friendlier and the idea of going local. Health', 'safety', 'immunity' and 'home' becoming centre stage with the pandemic, the brands were pushed to explore experiential and engagement driven campaigns enhancing sponsorship effectiveness on the Return On Investment in a sporting context.

Influence on Olympics Performance

Any Olympic Game more than 20 percent medals comes from Athletics and swimming. During Rio Olympic Games in 2016 there were total 971 medals to be won and 250 medals belonged to Athletics and Swimming competitions. Out of total 306 gold medals, 81 gold medals were to be won in these two events. Indian Athletes competed in 28 sports in the Rio Olympics 2016 of which eight sports leagues have been started where 52 gold medals were at stake. The proposed traditional and Olympic sporting leagues may bring more laurels for the country. Indian sporting performance at Olympics is attributed to multiple variables such as poor governance, insufficient infrastructure, lack of awareness, physical connectivity and health facilities in rural areas, training support and dedication. Sporting leagues have provided avenues to those who are keen to play and that would provide possibility for more medals for India in future Olympic Games.

Sports Audiences and Society

Sports viewers demand thrilling, exciting, analytical experience, either because of the game or through the technology used for sports broadcasting. The Cricket is not played between the 22 yards but has 35 Cameras set-up, view from every angle of the ground, slow motions and ultra-slow motions, augmented and virtual reality graphics, usage of buggy and spider cam to show the ariel and ground views to take the viewer inside the ground. The viewer is the king for the sports broadcaster and to keep engaging him/her for three hours T20 or seven hours one-day cricket match is the most important part. Not only during the game but before the start of the play, technology such as touch screen and graphics get used to analyze the game minutely. The fans of the game bring history to the sport with past records and future expectations from the players.

Viewers who are sitting at the home want to have a 360-degree view and complete viewing experience. The sports broadcasting technology helps in enhancing the experience and keep them engaged with the thrill of the game. Technology also help in administration of the game in a transparent and effective way. Umpires can make an accurate decision because of high end technologies used for review during broadcasting.

Mohit Singh brings March 27, 2020 story bringing Broadcast Audience Research Council of India (BARC) ratings for week 11 (March 14 to 20, 2020) for sports genre in India reveal up to 40 percent collapse in the gross impressions for the top five most-watched channels for the week. Broadcasters Audience Research Board (BARB) reported that the viewership of the IPL games surpassed the viewership of English Premier League (EPL) matches during IPL 2020 season. These clearly indicate global audiences for local league tournaments and increasing interest in sports as a genre. But the loss of local viewership was due to absence of live content. This also clearly suggest that sustaining audience interest is a critical challenge for all those involved in league business.

Way Ahead

Deloitte (2020) highlights five trends that will have the biggest impact on athletes, team and league executives, and players across the sports ecosystem: (1) the rise of women's sports, (2) the continued evolution of esports, (3) legalised sports betting, (4) college athletes maximising their short-term value, and (5) 5G/sports in the cloud.

The young population of India with 35 crore people in the age of 10 to 24 years of age, the increase of television audience and mobile phones greatly enhanced the viewership probability and it is equally associated with the biggest source of revenue. Another important factor is, non-television friendly sports can be played online and can be watched online too, so all the online audience can be drawn-in for cases such as Chess, mobile games and Esports.

The essential ingredients that sports bring are thrill, passion, speed, fight and competitive oppositions embedded in the broadcast. It can be concluded for certain that any sport which can be televised and can engage the audience on any platform, can start a professional sports league. The technology and its engaging aspect can play crucial role in spreading the passion for the sport. The scheduling of the event, available timing for the sports fans, association of music, celebrities, festival like surroundings enhance the mood of the audience and all these factors create an entertainment weekends or evening enjoyed with friends and families- onsite or off site on television screen at home, restaurants or resorts. Parties are being hosted around matches. Urban India is finding sports entertainment as new form of 'pass time'.

Existing sporting leagues have prepared a platform for upcoming sports leagues and template is set for the new sports leagues to enhance the culture of sports viewership in the country- outdoors as well as indoors, at home and in the stadiums. In May 2020, Danish football Team AGF Aarhus played matches to their fans through world's first grandstand via zoom due to Covid pandemic and this is the beginning of new era of sports broadcasting.

Digital sporting seems to be creating newer opportunities for sports exhibitions globally. Esports and E-experiences will impact the emotions of future generations, missing the sweat and the dust of sports arena!

References

- Ahluwalia, Harveen (2017), IPL viewership jumped 22.5% in 2017: BARC, Live Mint, June 02, 2017, URL: https://www.livemint.com/Consumer/Y8J13d9lObcYS7xFFcUXNI/IPL-viewership-jumped-225-in-2017-BARC.html
- Aiyar, Shankkar (2008), Lord of the League, Cover Story, India Today, June 16, 2008, URL: https://www.indiatoday.in/magazine/cover-story/story/20080616-lord-of-the-league-736534-2008-06-05
- Ali Qaiser Mohammad (2020), Why India's Sports Administrators Hate To Adopt A National Sports Development Code, Outlook India, 27 January 2020, URL: https://www.outlookindia.com/magazine/story/sports-news-why-indias-sports-administrators-hate-to-adopt-a-national-sports-development-code/302623
- Amin, Ruhail (2016), With New Identity, 'Delhi Sultans' All Set To Conquer Pro Wrestling Season 2, Business World, December 24, 2016, URL: http://www.businessworld.in/article/With-New-Identity-Delhi-Sultans-All-Set-To-Conquer-Pro-Wrestling-Season-2-/24-12-2016-110239/
- Andrews, D. L.; Jackson, S. J. (2001), Introduction: Sport celebrities, public culture, and private experience. In: Andrews, D. L.; Jackson, S. J., eds. Sport stars: the cultural politics of sporting celebrity (pp. 1-19). London: Rutledge.
- AP (2020) Pandemic could change landscape of minor league sports, The Times of India, May 30, 2020 URL: https://timesofindia.indiatimes.com/sports/more-sports/others/pandemic-could-change-landscape-of-minor-league-sports/articleshow/75707790.cms
- Appadurai, A. (1995), 'Playing with Modernity: The Decolonisation of Indian Cricket', in C.A. Breckenridge (ed.), Consuming Modernity: Public Culture in a South Asian World (Minneapolis, MN: University of Minnesota Press.
- Bansal, Shuchi (2017), Will Star India benefit from IPL media rights deal? September 7, 2017 URL: https://www.livemint.com/Opinion/YNX4ZRLWSl7NoCxpaSppRI/Will-Star-India-benefit-from-the-IPL-media-rights-deal.html

- Bapna, Amit (2019), The Inequality of Sports Leagues, Brand Equity, Economic Times, July 10, 2019 URL: https://brandequity.economictimes.indiatimes.com/news/business-of-brands/the-inequality-of-sports-leagues/70151397
- BARC Newsletter (2018), IPL Over the Years 2018, Broadcast Audience Research Council India, 2018, Newsletter, Issue 4, URL: https://www.barcindia.co.in/resources/IPL%20-%20Over%20the%20Years.pdf
- Bartlett, Roger, "The Science and medicine of cricket : an overview an update", Journal of Sports Sciences, Vol. 21, 2003, Issue 9, pp. 733-752 Published online 13 June 2018.
- Barua, Suhrid (2020), PBL 2020: How are franchise owners justified in spending 'big' on star players?, The Bridge, January 27, 2020, URL: https://thebridge.in/badminton/pbl-2020-how-franchise-owners-justified-spending-big-star-players/
- Basu Samyajit (2014), Stars embrace soccer through Indian Super League, Times of India, April 14, 2014, URL: https://timesofindia.indiatimes.com/sports/football/indian-super-league/top-stories/Stars-embrace-soccer-through-Indian-Super-League/articleshow/33712666.cms#write
- Best Media Info Bureau (2018), Sony Pictures Sports Network bags telecast rights for Pro Wrestling League Season 3, Best Media info, January 10, 2018, URL : https://bestmediainfo.com/2018/01/sony-pictures-sports-network-bags-telecast-rights-for-pro-wrestling-league-season-3/
- Best Media Info (2012), Record reach for IPL 5 Final; beats IPL 4 rating, Best Media info, June 7, 2012, URL : https://bestmediainfo.com/2012/06/record-reach-for-ipl-5-final-beats-ipl-4-rating/
- Bhat, Varada (2013), IPL -4 Final Scores a SIX on TV, Business Standard, January 20, 2013.
- Bhatia, Neeru (2020), Punting in a Pandemic, The Week, Vol. 38, No. 33, pp. 51-54, August 16, 2020.
- Bhattacharjya, Joy (2016), Pro-Kabbadi League teaches how to build a successful sports league, July 19,2016, The Economic Times, URL: https://economictimes.indiatimes.com/news/sports/pro-kabbadi-league-teaches-how-to-build-a-successful-sports league/articleshow/53441326.cms
- Bhattacharyya, Anushree (2018), Premier Badminton League expects to break even in FY20,Brand Equity, Economic Times, November 30, 2018, URL:https://brandequity.economictimes.indiatimes.com/news/media/premier-badminton-league-expects-to-boost-its-revenues/66874486
- Bhat, Varada (2013), Brand IPL comes under Cloud, Business Standard, January 21, 2013, URL: https://www.business-standard.com/article/management/brand-ipl-comes-under-a-cloud-112060100537_1.html
- Bindiya, Shefali (2020), IPL 2020 Advertising : 31 new categories, 162 brands advertising with Star Sports on IPL 2020, October 27, 2020, URL:

https://www.insidesport.co/ipl-2020-advertising-31-new-categories-162-brands-advertising-with-star-sports-on-ipl-2020/

- Bisoyi, Sujit Kumar (2019), Odisha gets its own ISL football club as Delhi Dynamos shift base to Bhubaneswar, Times of India, August 31, 2019, URL: https://timesofindia.indiatimes.com/sports/football/indian-super-league/top-stories/odisha-gets-its-own-isl-football-club-as-delhi-dynamos-shift-base-to-bhubaneswar/articleshow/70928674.cms
- Brown, Maury (2019), MLB sets record 107 billion in revenue for 2019, Forbes, December 21, 2019, URL: https://www.forbes.com/sites/maurybrown/2019/12/21/mlb-sees-record-107-billion-in-revenues-for-2019/#49a538305d78
- BS Web Team (2019), Prize money and eliminator schedule: Know about Pro Kabaddi 2019 playoffs, Business Standard, October 13, 2019, URL: https://www.business-standard.com/article/sports/prize-money-and-eliminator-schedule-know-about-pro-kabaddi-2019-playoffs-119101200464_1.html#:~:text=Meanwhile%2C%20the%20pro%20kabaddi%20league,will%20receive%20Rs%201.8%20crore.
- Business Standard (2015), Pro Wrestling League teams unveiled, Business Standard, November 21, 2015, URL: https://www.business-standard.com/article/news-ians/pro-wrestling-league-teams-unveiled-115112100365_1.html
- Business Wire India (2014), American Appraisal Releases IPL Brand Evaluation Report 2014, Business Wire India, February 11, 2014, URL: https://www.businesswireindia.com/american-appraisal-releases-ipl-brand-evaluation-report-2014-38253.html
- Cain, L P and D D Haddock (2005), Similar Economic Histories, Different Industrial Structures: Transatlantic Contrasts in the Evolution of Professional Sports Leagues. Journal of Economic History, 65(4), p. 1116-1147.
- Carter, Jamie (2019), 10 tech innovations we saw at the Cricket World Cup, July 29, 2019 URL: https://www.techradar.com/in/news/10-tech-innovations-we-saw-at-the-cricket-world-cup
- Chilkoti, Avantika (2013), India's Cricket league gets its brand value back, Financial Times, April 25, 2013, URL: https://www.ft.com/content/755c103b-fee1-3a15-8384-dea83a1afdab
- Coakley, Jay (2011), Ideology does not just happen: Sports and Neoliberalism, Curitiba, vol. 1, no. 1, pp. 67-84, September 2011 URL: https://www.researchgate.net/profile/Jay_Coakley/publication/236001299
- Cricinfo Staff (2008), Big business and Bollywood grab stakes in IPL, January 24, 2008, URL:https://www.espncricinfo.com/story/_/id/20427511/ipl-announces-franchise-owners
- Cricket 365 (2018), News Article, April 2018, "Advanced Technologies Used In Cricket Games" URL: https://www.cricket365.com/latest-news/advanced-technologies-used-in-cricket-games/

- Dasgupta, Pritha Mitra (2015), MSM wins broadcast rights of Pro Wrestling League, Brand Equity, Economic Times, November 16, 2015, URL : https://brandequity.economictimes.indiatimes.com/news/media/msm-wins-broadcast-rights-of-pro-wrestling-league/49796918
- David, Turney (2017), Professional sports franchise valuation URL: https://www.toptal.com/finance/mergers-and-acquisitions/sports-franchise-valuation
- DC Chitrangada (2018), https://www.mykhel.com/badminton/pbl-2018-19-bengaluru-raptors-team-player-profiles-105390.html, My Khel, December 10, 2018, URL: https://www.mykhel.com/badminton/pbl-2018-19-bengaluru-raptors-team-player-profiles-105390.html
- Deloitte (2020) 2020 Sports Industry Outlook, Deloitte Centre for Technology, Media, and Telecommunication, URL: https://www2.deloitte.com/us/en/pages/technology-media-and-telecommunications/articles/sports-business-trends-disruption.html
- Dharamshi, Manan (2020), Premier Badminton League 2020: PBL 2020, Schedule, Teams, Sponsors, Kreedon.com, January 21, 2020, URL:https://www.kreedon.com/premier-badminton-league-2020-pbl-2020/
- Dubey, Abhishek (2010), The IPL Story: Cricket, Glamour and Big Money, Pearson Education India, Delhi.
- Duff & Phelps (2017), IPL: The Decade Edition : A concise report on brand values in the Indian Premier League, Duff & Phelps, August 2017, URL:https://www.duffandphelps.com/-/media/assets/pdfs/news/valuation-services/ipl-the-decade-edition-1.pdf
- Duggal, Saurabh and Sandip Sikdar (2020), Uncertainty plagues nation's smaller leagues, April 28, 2020 URL: https://www.hindustantimes.com/other-sports/covid-19-impact-players-on-back-foot-uncertainty-plagues-nation-s-smaller-leagues/story-x8u4pgXfTRSsMVOz9soNIO.html
- Economic Times Wealth (2017), This is how Shah Rukh Khan earns and spends the money, May 22, 2017, URL: https://economictimes.indiatimes.com/wealth/invest/this-is-how-shah-rukh-khan-earns-and-spends-the-money/a-self-made-star/slideshow/58790707.cms
- Engineer, Tariq (2011), TV ratings plunge, but viewership rises, 06-May-2011, URL: URL : https://www.espncricinfo.com/story/_/id/22443538/indian-premier-league-2011-tv-ratings-plunge,-viewership-rises
- Espncricinfo Staff (2015), India Cements shareholders to get CSK shares, February 25, 2012, URL:https://www.espncricinfo.com/story/_/id/21294394/india-cements-shareholders-get-csk-shares
- ET BrandEquity (2020), Experiential sports marketing: 'Home as a new playground', August 31, 2020, URL: https://brandequity.economictimes.indiatimes.com/news/marketing/experiential-sports-marketing-home-as-a-new-playground/77844175

- ET Bureau (2011), Adidas India head Andreas Gellner who shares lessons he learnt from Indian consumers, Economic Times, April 10, 2011 URL: https://economictimes.indiatimes.com/industry/cons-products/garments-/-textiles/adidas-india-head-andreas-gellnerwho-shares-lessons-he-learnt-from-indian-consumers/articleshow/7929337.cms
- ET Online (2018), Delhi Daredevils IPL team renamed as Delhi Capitals, December 4, 2018, URL: https://m.economictimes.com/news/sports/delhi-daredevils-ipl-team-renamed-as-delhi-capitals/articleshow/66938183.cms
- Evens, T., Iosifidis, P., Smith, P. (2013), The Sports Broadcasting Market. In: The Political Economy of Television Sports Rights. Palgrave Global Media Policy and Business. Palgrave Macmillan, London. https://doi.org/10.1057/9781137360342_3
- FICCI-EY (2020), The Era of Consumer A.R.T. Acquition Retention Transaction, URL: http://ficci.in/spdocument/23200/FICCI-EY-Report-media-and-entertainment-2020.pdf
- Gemmell, Jon (2018), Cricket's Changing Ethos: Nobles, Nationalists and the IPL (Global Culture and Sport Series), Palgrave Macmillan, London.
- Gough, Christina (2019), Biggest prize money in sports worldwide in 2019, Statista, November 22, 2019, URL: https://www.statista.com/statistics/754438/highest-paid-sports-events/
- Gramsci, A. (1971), Selections from the prison notebook (Q. Hoare and G. N. Smith, trans). New York: International Publishers (original work published in 1947).
- Guha, Ramachandra (1998), 'Cricket and Politics in Colonial India', Past and Present, Nov. 1998; A Corner of a Foreign Field: The Indian History of a British Sport (Delhi: Picador, 2002).
- Guha, Ray Shantanu (2016), Fixed! Cash and Corruption in Cricket, HarperSport, New Delhi.
- Gupta, Varun, N Santosh (2016), Indian Premier League 2016 Brand Value Study, Duff & Phelps, June 27, 2016, URL : https://duffandphelps.com/insights/publications/valuation/indian-premier-league-brand-value-report-june-2016
- Gupta, Varun, N Santosh (2019), Duff & Phelps Launches IPL Brand Valuation Report 2019, Duff & Phelps, September 20, 2019, URL: https://www.duffandphelps.com/insights/publications/valuation/ipl-brand-valuation-report-2019
- Hindustan Times (2017), Sachin Tendulkar now becomes co-owner of a Pro Kabaddi League team, Hindustan Times, May 12, 2017, URL: https://www.hindustantimes.com/other-sports/sachin-tendulkar-among-new-owners-in-pro-kabaddi-league/story-INkCZEadLKVnN60IIeShbK.html
- Hoover, Mark (2019), Big Bout Indian Boxing League: Odisha Warriors scent maiden victory after taking 2-0 lead over Brawlers, My Khel, December 8, 2019, URL:https://www.mykhel.com/more-sports/big-bout-

indian-boxing-league-odisha-warriors-scent-maiden-victory-brawlers-133246.html

- Hoover, Mark (2020), Big Bout Indian Boxing League: Odisha Warriors scent maiden victory after taking 2-0 lead over Brawlers,Mykhel.com, December 8, 2019, URL: https://www.mykhel.com/more-sports/big-bout-indian-boxing-league-odisha-warriors-scent-maiden-victory-brawlers-133246.html
- HT Correspondent (2019), IPL 2020: Five IPL teams that are no longer part of Indian Premier League, Hindustan Times, November 27, 2019, URL: https://www.hindustantimes.com/cricket/ipl-2020-five-ipl-teams-that-are-no-longer-part-of-indian-premier-league/story-3vYMbJbqDftCUOQOdcas0N.html
- India Today Web Desk (2018), Tendulkar sells stakes in Kerala Blasters, says will cherish experience forever, India Today, September 16, 2018, URL: https://www.indiatoday.in/sports/football/story/sachin-tendulkar-stakes-kerala-blasters-indian-super-league-1341179-2018-09-16
- India Today Web Desk (2019), How Hardik Pandya and KL Rahul got into trouble for Koffee with Karan: A timeline, India Today, January 13, 2019 URL: https://www.indiatoday.in/sports/cricket/story/hardik-pandya-kl-rahul-koffee-with-karan-controversy-timeline-1430046-2019-01-13
- Indian Express (2016), Film stars Chiranjeevi, Akkineni Nagarjuna join Sachin Tendulkar as co-owners of Kerala Blasters, Indian Express, June 1, 2016, URL:https://indianexpress.com/article/sports/football/film-stars-join-sachin-tendulkar-as-co-owners-of-kerala-blasters-2829184/
- Indian Express (2018), Pro Wrestling League: Mumbai Maharathi make U-turn hours after pulling out, Indian Express, January 18, 2018, URL: https://indianexpress.com/article/sports/sport-others/pro-wrestling-league-mumbai-maharathi-make-u-turn-hours-after-pulling-out-5030253/
- Insidesport (2018), U Mumba owner alleges Star India has conflict of interest in PKL: Report, December 3, 2018, URL: https://www.insidesport.co/u-mumba-owner-alleges-star-india-has-conflict-of-interest-in-pkl-report/
- IYSPE (2005) Report on the International Year of Sport and Physical Education, Ingrid Beutler (ed.), United Nations, Geneva.
- Jagannathan, KT, and Vijaykumar Sanjay (2015), CSK Ltd. to be owned by one lakh shareholders, The Hindu, February 11, 2015, URL:https://www.thehindu.com/sport/cricket/india-cements-board-approves-csk-transfer-to-subsidiary/article6883237.ece
- Kaul, Vivek (2016), India's Big Government: The intrusive state and how it's hurting us, Equitymaster Agora Research Private Limited, Mumbai.
- Keerthivasan, K (2019), Premier Badminton League: It will now be Chennai Superstarz, The Hindu, November 27, 2019, URL: https://

www.thehindu.com/sport/other-sports/premier-badminton-league-it-will-now-be-chennai-superstarz/article30092867.ece

- Khan Yusuf (2019), These are the 10 most valuable sports franchises in the world in 2019, Business Insider India, July 24, 2019.
- Koppett Leonard (1994), Sports illusion, Sports Reality: A Reporter's view of Sports, Journalism and Society, University of Illinois Press, Urbana and Chicago.
- KPMG Report (2016), The Business of Sports, KPMG, September, 2016, URL:https://assets.kpmg/content/dam/kpmg/in/pdf/2016/09/the-business-of-sports.pdf
- KPMG-IFSG (2019), The evolving landscape of sports gaming in India, KPMG and Indian Federation of Sports Gaming, March 2019, URL: https://home.kpmg/in/en/home/insights/2019/03/online-gaming-india-fantasy-sports.html
- Kumar Jain, Piyush & Chakrawati Rajesh, "Improvement in Hot Spot Technology in Cricket", International Journal of Scientific & Engineering Research, Volume 5, Issue 10, October-2014 257 ISSN 2229-5518
- Laghate, Gaurav (2016), 121 million viewers tuned in for IPL 9 final, Economic Times, June 10, 2016, URL: https://economictimes.indiatimes.com/industry/media/entertainment/media/121-million-viewers-tuned-in-for-ipl-9-final/articleshow/52681013.cms
- Laghate, Gaurav (2017a), ₹ 54.5 crore per match is not insane, look at it in right context: Star India CEO Uday Shankar, Economic Times, September 5, 2017, URL : https://economictimes.indiatimes.com/industry/media/entertainment/media/star-india-wins- ipl-media-rights-for-rs-16347-5-crore-for-5-years/articleshow/60359780.cms
- Laghate, Gaurav (2017b), Badminton League gets 4 sponsors, 2 more teams, Economic Times, December 1, 2017,URL:https://economictimes.indiatimes.com/news/sports/badminton-league-gets-4-sponsors-2-more-teams/articleshow/62060799.cms
- Laghate, Gaurav (2019), IPL 2019 breaks viewership records, Economic Times, May 24, 2019, URL:https://economictimes.indiatimes.com/news/sports/ipl-2019-breaks-viewership-records/articleshow/69483861.cms
- Laghate, Gaurav (2019), IPL brand valuation soars 13.5% to ₹ 47,500 crore: Duff & Phelps, Economic Times, September 20, 2019, URL:https://economictimes.indiatimes.com/news/sports/ipl-brand-valuation-soars-13-5-to-rs-47500-crore-duff-phelps/articleshow/71197984.cms
- Laghate, Gaurav (2019), We have pressed reboot button after coming as equal owners in Delhi Capitals: Parth Jindal, Economic Times, March 14, 2019, URL:https://economictimes.indiatimes.com/news/sports/willing-to-buy-out-gmr-in-delhi-ipl-team-at-right-price-parth-jindal/articleshow/68402498.cms

- Laghate, Gaurav (2020), Indian Sports Sponsorship Crosses Rs. 9000 Crore Mark in 2019, March 12, 2020, Economic Times, URL: https://economictimes.indiatimes.com/industry/services/ advertising/ indian-sports-sponsorship-crosses-rs-9000-crore-mark-in-2019-groupm-esp/articleshow/74594615.cms
- Laghate, Gaurav (2020), Kolkata based start up to begin franchise format Quiz League, Economic Times, June 16, 2020, URL: https://economictimes.indiatimes.com/small-biz/startups/newsbuzz/kolkata-based-startup-to-begin-franchise-format-quiz-league/articleshow/76404488.cms
- Laghate, Gaurav (2019), Pro Volleyball signs Nippon Paint as associate sponsor for first two seasons, Economic Times, January 2, 2019,. URL: https://economictimes.indiatimes.com/news/sports/pro-volleyball-signs-nippon-paint-as-associate-sponsor-for-first-two-seasons/articleshow/67352234.cms
- Laghate, Gaurav, Ravi Teja Sharma (2016), IPL brand valuation soars to $4.16 billion: Duff & Phelps, Economic Times, June 27, 2016, URL: https://economictimes.indiatimes.com/industry/services/advertising/ipl-brand-valuation-soars-to-4-16-billion-duff-phelps/articleshow/52930766.cms
- Lange David (2020) Highest Paid Sports events wondwide 2019, November 26, 2020 URL: https://www.statista.com/statistics/754438/highest-paid-sports-events/
- Lasrado, Svetlana (2014), Bengaluru Bulls gear up for Pro Kabbadi League, The New Indian Express, July 21, 2014, URL: https://www.newindianexpress.com/cities/bengaluru/2014/jul/21/Bengaluru-Bulls-gear-up-for-Pro-Kabbadi-League-638266.html
- Lokapally, Vijay (2018), "Technology's role in cricket today", The Hindu, April 17, 2018, URL: https://www.thehindu.com/sci-tech/technology/techs-in-the-crease/article23558187.ece
- Louis, Bosshart & Lea Hellmuller, "Sportainment : Sports & Entertainment", Communication Research Trends, Volume 28, (2009) No. 2 - (pp. 17-18)
- Maddox, Tina, "The 6 coolest tech innovations being used at the 2018 FIFA World Cup" Tech Republic, July 13, 2018; URL: https://www.techrepublic.com/article/the-6-coolest-tech-innovations-being-used-at-the-2018-fifa-world-cup/
- Malu, Jatin (2020), Who Owns RCB? United Spirits' Initial Investment In The IPL Team And Current Brand Value, Republic World, April 10, 2020,URL: https://www.republicworld.com/sports-news/cricket-news/who-owns-rcb-united-spirits-initial-investment-current-brand-value-ipl.html
- Malvania, Urvi (2015), IPL fever: KKR beats CSK in brand value race, Business Standard, April 15, 2015, URL : https://www.business-standard.com/article/companies/ipl-fever-kkr-beats-csk-in-brand-value-race-115041401009_1.html

- Malvania, Urvi (2016), Star Sports title sponsor of Premier Badminton League, Business Standard, January 2, 2016, URL: https://www.business-standard.com/article/current-affairs/star-sports-is-title-sponsor-of-revamped-premier-badminton-league-116010100460_1.html
- Mazumdar, Boria (2018), Rise and Fall of Lalit Modi from Creating IPL to eventual Exile, March 27, 2018, Economic Times, URL: https://economictimes.indiatimes.com/news/sports/rise-and-fall-of-lalit-modi-from-creating-ipl-to-eventual-exile/articleshow/63475073.cms
- Mccleary, Meredith (2019), Politics and Sports: A Long and Complicated Relationship, International Affairs, North Eastern Political Review, February 26, 2019, URL: https://www.nupoliticalreview.com/2019/02/26/politics-and-sports-a-long-and-complicated-relationship/
- Menon, D Bindu (2018), More Brands Back ISL In Season 3, The Hindu Business Line, January 16, 2018, URL:https://www.thehindubusinessline.com/news/sports/more-brands-back-isl-in-season-3/article9184945.ece
- Mergulhao, Marcus (2014), ISL offers ₹ 15 crore in prize money, The Times of India, August 17, 2014, URL:https://timesofindia.indiatimes.com/city/goa/ISL-offers-Rs-15-crore-in-prize- money/articleshow/40318361.cms
- Mills, James (2005) ed., Subaltern Sports- Politics and Sports in South Asia, Anthem Press, London.
- Mishra, Saurabh (2015), Two leagues one goal: should India's two leagues merge to improve Indian football? Law in Sport, August 27, 2015, URL: https://www.lawinsport.com/topics/item/two-leagues-one-goal-should-india-s-two-leagues-merge-to-improve-indian-football
- Money Control (2019), IPL 2019: Meet the owners of the 8 teams taking the field in season 12, Money Control.com, March 24, 2019,URL: https://www.moneycontrol.com/news/trends/sports-trends/ipl-2019-meet-the-owners-of-the-8-teams-taking-the-field-in-season-12-2542331.html
- Morgan, William (2006), Why Sports Morally Matters, Routledge, New York.
- Murray Bruce, K. (2002), The Sports Boycott and Cricket: The Cancellation of the 1970 South African Tour of England, South African Historical Journal, 46:1, 219-249, DOI: 10.1080/02582470208671425
- N Santosh (2020), Duff & Phelps IPL Brand Valuation Report Featured in Financial Times, Duffe & Phelps, April 24, 2020, URL: https://www.duffandphelps.com/about-us/news/ipl-brand-valuation-report-featured-financial-times
- Nair, Sangeeta (2019), Sports Ministry constitutes new committee to review draft of National Code for Good governance in Sports, Jagran Josh, November 28, 2019, URL: https://www.jagranjosh.com/current-affairs/sports-ministry-constitutes-new-committee-to-review-draft-of-national-code-for-good-governance-in-sports-1574926997-1

- Nandy, Ashis (2000), The Tao of Cricket: On Games of Destiny and the Destiny of Games, Oxford India Paperbacks, New Delhi.
- News Report, (2013), ₹ 2.5 crore prize money for HIL winners, The Times of India, January 28, 2013 URL: https://timesofindia.indiatimes.com/sports/hockey/hockey-india-league/top-stories/Rs-2-5-crore-prize-money-for-HIL-winners/articleshow/18223366.cms
- NewsX YouTube Channel (2019), NE Rhinos Owner Sanjive Narain with Boxer Mandeep Singh Speaks to NewsX, NewsX, December 8, 2019, URL: https://www.youtube.com/watch?v=Di8XRcfKjCk
- NewsX YouTube Channel (2019), Big Bout Boxing League: Bombay Bullets Owner Deepak Speaks to NewsX, NewX TV News Channel, December 17, 2019, URL: https://www.youtube.com/watch?v=r2gmdWjo5kw
- NewsX YouTube Channel (2019), Bombay Bullets Owner Colonel Dev Negi speaks to NewsX on Big Bout League, NewX TV News Channel, December 5, 2019, URL: https://www.youtube.com/watch?v=7wIYBlXHfTU
- NewsX YouTube Channel (2019), Punjab Panthers Owner Dilip Pandey speaks to NewsX on Big Bout League, NewX TV News Channel, December 5, 2019, URL: https://www.youtube.com/watch?v=o0rulw3SNFE&list=UUytSP0M0Jdnw6qIy3Y-nTig&index=73
- NewsX YouTube channel (2019), Big Bout League: Odisha Warriors owner Aditya Goyal speaks to NewsX, NewsX, December 17, 2019, URL : https://www.youtube.com/watch?v=7m4q81-n008
- Ninan, Susan (2017), All you need to know about Ultimate Table Tennis, ESPN.in, July 11, 2017, URL: https://www.espn.in/espn/story/_/id/19962661/ultimate-table-tennis-rules-teams-format-dates-schedule-players-prize-money
- Noll, Roger, G. (2007), Broadcasting and Team Sports , Stanford Institute for Economic Policy Research , Stanford University, February, 2007, URL: https://siepr.stanford.edu/sites/default/files/publications/06-16_0.pdf
- Noll, Roger & Patel, Dharmesh. (2003), The Organisation of Sports Leagues. Oxford Review of Economic Policy. 19. 530-551. 10.1093/oxrep/19.4.530.
- Noorbhai, M.H. & Noakes, T.D., (2015) "Advances in cricket in the 21century: Science, performance and Technology" African Journal for Physical, Health Education, Recreation and Dance (AJPHERD) Volume 21(4:2), December 2015, pp. 1310-1320.
- Official YouTube Channel (2017), UP Dangal Owner Sunny Katyal Talks about the Team, Investors Clinic You Tube Channel, January 9, 2017, https://www.youtube.com/watch?v=QHPaCs5_6XE
- Official YouTube Channel of Chennai Superstarz (2019), Behind The Scenes: Short Interview with owners Aditya Meesala and R. Sivakumar, December 17, 2019

- Official YouTube Channel of Pro Wrestling League (2017), Bobby Deol Co-Owner of NCR Punjab Royals at Pro Wrestling League Season 2, You Tube channel, Pro Wrestling League, January 18, 2017, URL
- Official YouTube Channel of Pro Wrestling League (2019), PWL 4: Owner of Winner Team Haryana Hammers Goldy Behl shows his enthusiasm after the victory, You Tube channel, February 1, 2019
- Pande Bhanu (2012), IPL impact: 5 new sports leagues come up in 18 months, non-cricket sports have no dearth of sponsors, March 12, 2012, Economic Times, URL: https://economictimes.indiatimes.com/news/company/corporate-trends/ipl-impact-5-new-sports-leagues-come-up-in-18-months-non-cricket-sports-have-no-dearth-of-sponsors/ articleshow / 12225965.cms
- Press Release, November 28, 2019, CFG acquires majority stake in Indian Super League's Mumbai City FC,URL: https://www.cityfootballgroup.com/information-resource/news-and-press-packs/cfg-acquires-majority-stake-in-indian-super-league-s-mumbai-city-fc/
- Press Trust of India (2013), ₹ 2.5 crore prize money for HIL winners, Times of India, January 28, 2013, URL:https://timesofindia.indiatimes.com/sports/hockey/hockey-india-league/top-stories/Rs-2-5-crore-prize-money-for-HIL-winners/articleshow/18223366.cms
- Press Trust of India (2014), DEN Network give up 25% Stake in Delhi Dynamos, PTI News, November 16, URL: http://ptinews.com/news/8085538_DEN-Networks-give-up-25—stake-in-Delhi-Dynamos-
- Press Trust of India (2019), PBL, PWL owners join hands to launch 'Big Bout - Indian Boxing League,' to feature top boxers like Mary Kom, Amit Panghal, First Post, November 15, 2019,URL:https://www.firstpost.com/sports/pbl-pwl-owners-join-hands-to-launch-big-bout-indian-boxing-league-to-feature-top-boxers-like-mary-kom-amit-panghal-7659081.html
- PricewaterhouseCoopers (2011), Changing the Game- Outlook for the global sports market 2015, Price waterhousecoopers, December 2011, URL: www.pwc.com/sportsoutlook
- Proman, Michael (2019) The future of sports tech: Here's where investors are placing their bets, October 2, 2019, URL: https://techcrunch.com/2019/10/01/the-future-of-sports-tech-heres-where-investors-are-placing-their-bets/
- Purandare Kunal (2019), Table tennis gets IPL-style flourish, Forbes India, July 25 2019, URL: https://www.forbesindia.com/article/special/table-tennis-gets-iplstyle-flourish/54519/1#:~:text=The%20runners%2Dup%20will%20get,awards%20of%20Rs25%20lakh%20too.
- Raghvendra, Nandini (2014), Dabang Delhi owner Radha Kapoor on her plans for Pro-Kabaddi League players, Economic Times, July 31, 2014, URL :https://economictimes.indiatimes.com/magazines/panache/dabang-

delhi-owner-radha-kapoor-on-her-plans-for-pro-kabaddi-league-players/articleshow/39339526.cms?from=mdr

- Raghvendra, Nandini, Sharma, Ravi Teja (2015), IPL 8 final was watched by 49.4 million people in 20.7 million homes: BARC, Economic Times, June 4, 2015, URL: https://economictimes.indiatimes.com/industry/media/entertainment/media/ipl-8-final-was-watched-by-49-4-million-people-in-20-7-million-homes-barc/articleshow/47543472.cms?from=mdr
- Raj, Rohan (2015), "Confessions corner! The untold story of an IPL cheerleader". India Today, URL: https://www.indiatoday.in/sports/ipl-2015/story/confessions-corner-troubles-of-being-an-ipl-8-cheerleader-reddit-252140-2015-05-09
- Ranjan, Prem (2019), PKL 2019 Owners: Pro Kabaddi League Team Owner, Captain and Coach Name List, Isports league, June 26 , 2019, URL : https://www.isportsleague.com/pro-kabaddi-league-team-owner-list/
- Reed, Adam (2019), European soccer posts record revenues with the English Premier League leading the way, CNBC, May 30, 2019, URL: https://www.cnbc.com/2019/05/30/european-soccer-posts-record-revenues-as-epl-dominates-deloitte.html
- Saini, Aakash (2020), Who Owns Rajasthan Royals? Owners Stake, Initial Investment and Team's Brand Value, April 13, 2020, URL: https://www.republicworld.com/sports-news/cricket-news/who-owns-rajasthan-royals-owners-net-worth-and-teams-brand-value.html
- Saini, Aakash (2020), Who Owns Kings XI Punjab? All About The IPL Team's 4 Owners And Its Increased Brand Value, Republic World, April 10, 2020, URL: https://www.republicworld.com/sports-news/cricket-news/who-owns-kings-xi-punjab-owners-combined-net-worth-teams-brand-value.html
- Scroll Staff (2020), Indian Football: ISL's table toppers to be awarded league winners shield, Cash Prize of 50 Lakh, Scroll.in, February 19, 2020, URL: https://scroll.in/field/953666/indian-football-isls-table-toppers-to-be-awarded-league-winners-shield-cash-prize-of-rs-50-lakh
- Sekhari, Gaurav Desh (2016), Not Out! The Incredible Story of the Indian Premier League, Penguin Random House, New Delhi.
- Senthil, Anjana (2019), PBL takes cue from other leagues, sets up Anti-Corruption Unit (ACU), SportStar The Hindu, January 12, 2019, URL:https://sportstar.thehindu.com/badminton/premier-badminton-league-anti-corruption-unit-atul-pande-managing-director-sportzlive/article25980520.ece
- Shah, Ruchika (2019), Sports Leagues: Games that they play, Forbes India, 30 May, 2019 published in June 7, 2019 issue, URL: https://www.forbesindia.com/article/sports-special/sports-leagues-games-that-they-play/53745/1

- Sharan, Anita (2009), IPL finals drew this year's highest TV viewership, Hindustan Times, May 25, 2009, URL: https://www.hindustantimes.com/business/ipl-finals-drew-this-year-s-highest-tv-viewership/story-qS2LQooEzRuVyzaGc8ApJK.html
- Sharan Anita (2011), IPL 4 pales in comparison to last year, Hindustan Times, May 19, 2011, URL:https://www.hindustantimes.com/cricket/ipl-4-pales-in-comparison-to-last-year/story-EFPKOKRQXHqcIWAGMytixH.html
- Sharma, Rajender (2020), IPL 2020: Cancellation to hit brand value by up to $1bn, reveals report, Inside Sport, March 21, 2020, URL: https://www.insidesport.co/ipl-2020-cancellation-to-hit-brand-value-by-up-to-1bn-reveals-report/
- Shergold, Adam (2020), 40 players, three VAR, four doping controllers and 130 media... How Premier League's 'ghost games' will look when matches resume behind closed doors once coronavirus suspension is lifted, Daily Mail online, UK, April 27, 2020, URL:https://www.dailymail.co.uk/sport/sportsnews/article-8260281/Coronavirus-UK-Premier-League-estimates-300-people-needed-match.html
- Shukla, Deepshikha (2019), Technologies that have transformed the sports experience, June 19, 2019 URL: https://ace.electronicsforu.com/estyle/technologies-transformed-sports-experience/
- Singh Mohit (2020) BARC Ratings: Sports genre biggest loser in absence off live content, March 27, 2020, URL: insidesport.co/barc_rating_sports_genre_biggest_loser_in_absence_off_live_content.
- Singh, Rajiv (2013), How IPL propelled India Cements, GMR Group, Muthoot Finance into a bigger league, ET Bureau, The Economic Times, March 24, 2013, URL: https://economictimes.indiatimes.com/news/company/corporate-trends/how-ipl-propelled-india-cements-gmr-group-muthoot-finance-into-a-bigger-eague/articleshow/19153973.cms
- Singh, Ujwal (2019), UTT 2019 player draft: Sharath Kamal roped in by Chennai Lions, Manika Batra to play for Mavericks Kolkata, First Post, June 13, 2019, URL: https://www.firstpost.com/sports/utt-2019-player-draft-sharath-kamal-roped-in-by-chennai-lions-manika-batra-to-play-for-mavericks-kolkata-6809411.html
- Sinha Ashish (2013), Record TV viewership generated for semi-final match of IPL 2, Business Standard, January 19, 2013, URL: https://www.business-standard.com/article/companies/record-tv-viewership-generated-for-semi-final-match-of-ipl-2-109052500012_1.html
- Special Correspondent (2014), I-League remains priority: Jerome, telegraphindia.com, published on 16 October 2014, viewed on 7 August 2015, URL: https://www.telegraphindia.com/1141016/jsp/sports/story_18931741.jsp

- Sport NDTV (2014), Indian Premier League 7 most popular on TV, social media, NDTV, July 7, 2014, URL :https://sports.ndtv.com/indian-premier-league-2014/indian-premier-league-7-most-popular-on-tv-social-media-1518136
- Sportstar (2020), Sports Sponsorship surges to Rs. 9000 Crores in India, March 14, 2020, URL: https://sportstar.thehindu.com/other-sports/sports-sponsorship-world-cup-2019-kohli-dhoni-mary-kom-hima-das/article31069495.ece
- SportStar (2020), BCCI chief Ganguly named as one of ATK-Mohun Bagan directors, SportStar The Hindu, July 5, 2020, URL: https://sportstar.thehindu.com/football/sourav-ganguly-bcci-president-named-atk-mohun-bagan-board-of-directors/article31995028.ece#
- Sportstar (2019), PWL: Do-or-die match for UP Dangal against Bajrang's Punjab Royals, Sport Star, The Hindu, January 28, 2019, URL: https://sportstar.thehindu.com/wrestling/pro-wrestling-league-2019/pwl-do-or-die-match-for-up-dangal-against-bajrangs-punjab-royals/article26111523.ece
- Srinivas, Alam and TR Vivek (2009), IPL- an Inside Story: Cricket & Commerce, Roli books, New Delhi.
- Staudohar, P A and James A Mangan (1991), ed. The Business of Professional Sports, University of Illinois Press, Urbana and Chicago.
- Stretch Richard, Bartlett Roger and Davids Keith (2000) "A review of batting in men's cricket", Journal of Sports Sciences, Vol. 18, pp. 931-949.
- Subrahmanyam, VV (2019), ISL 2019-20: Film star Rana Daggubati new stakeholder of Hyderabad FC, Sportstar, The Hindu, October 24, 2019, URL:https://sportstar.thehindu.com/football/isl/isl-news/isl-2019-20-hyderabad-fc-rana-daggubati-stakeholder-kamaljit-singh-indian-super-league/article29789759.ece
- Tagore, Vijay (2019), KXIP co-owner Mohit Burman: It's Ness Wadia's personal matte and nothing to do with Kings XI franchise, Pune Mirror, May 5, 2019, URL:https://punemirror.indiatimes.com/sport/cricket/kxip-co-owner-says-its-nesss-personal-matter/articleshow/69180420.cms
- Team Sportstar (2016), Delhi Dynamos ropes in GMS-led Wall Street Investments, Sports Star, The Hindu, October 08, 2016, URL: https://sportstar.thehindu.com/football/isl/delhi-dynamos-ropes-in-gmsled-wall-street-investments/article9201982.ece
- Team Sportstar (2019), MI vs CSK IPL final: Winner to pocket ₹ 20 crore, more than four times the 2008 prize money, Sportstar, The Hindu, May 12, 2019, URL: https://sportstar.thehindu.com/cricket/ipl/ipl-2019-final-mi-csk-prize-money-winner-runner-up-dhoni-rohit-sharma/article27108201.ece
- Team SportStar (2020), Mohun Bagan, ATK announce merger; to play ISL next season, SportStar, The Hindu, January 16, 2020, URL: https://

sportstar.thehindu.com/football/mohun-bagan-atk-merger-official-rpsg-group-majority-stake-isl-ileague-indian-football-news/article30576195.ece

- Tewari Saumya (2018), IPL final viewership jumps 41% to 55.6 mn impressions on TV, Live Mint, June 8, 2018, URL: https://www.livemint.com/Sports/fGCIL5JxhO2HEe0LCFhWhM/IPL-final-viewership-jumps-41-to-556-mn-impressions-on-TV.html
- Tewari, Saumya (2020), Sports rights in India expected to touch $1.3 bn by 2024, Live Mint, March 6, 2020, URL: https://www.livemint.com/industry/advertising/sports-rights-in-india-expected-to-touch-1-3-bn-by-2024-11583490221074.html
- Thakue, Vishal & Kumar, Pravin: "A Case Study: Technological advancement in cricket".
- The Fake IPL Player (2010), The Game Changers- Cricket Meets Bollywood and the Bog that saw it all, Harper Collins, New Delhi.
- The Fan Garage (2015), PWL unveils the names and owners of the 6 franchises for the inaugural edition, November 21, 2015, URL: https://thefangarage.com/articles/2606-pwl-unveils-the-names-and-owners-of-the-6-franchises-for-the-inaugural-edition
- The Financial Express (2020), Esports at the Olympics- online gaming is gaining momentum to be taken seriously as a sport, February 23, 2020 URL: https://www.financialexpress.com/lifestyle/esports-at-the-olympics-professional-online-gaming-is-gaining-momentum-to-be-taken-seriously-as-a-sport/1876113/
- The Hindu (2019), Champions Boat League: Kerala goes the way of IPL, renames nine popular boat Clubs, August 22, 2019, URL: https://www.thehindu.com/news/national/kerala/knights-warriors-to-race-in-boat-league/article29214987.ece
- Times of India (2019), Hyderabad FC replace struggling FC Pune City as new ISL franchise, Times of India, August 27, 2019, URL: https://timesofindia.indiatimes.com/sports/football/indian-super-league/top-stories/hyderabad-fc-replace-struggling-fc-pune-city-as-new-isl-franchise/articleshow/70862303.cms
- Times of India (2019), Rajasthan Royals owner set to sell stakes, big business houses expected to bid, Times of India, January 17, 2019, URL: https://timesofindia.indiatimes.com/sports/cricket/ipl/top-stories/rajasthan-royals-owner-set-to-sell-stakes-big-business-houses-expected-to-bid/articleshow/67574182.cms
- Tiwary, Rajesh (2017), Remembering Indian Cricket League, the 'rebel' that led to IPL would have turned 10 today, November 30, 2017 URL: https://www.firstpost.com/firstcricket/sports-news/remembering-indian-cricket-league-the-rebel-that-led-to-ipl-would-have-turned-10-today-4235115.html

- TJ Mathewson (2019), TV is biggest driver in global sport league revenue, Global sports matters, March 7, 2019 Business, https://globalsportmatters.com/business/2019/03/07/tv-is-biggest-driver-in-global-sport-league-revenue/
- Tripathi, Sanjeev & Ankur Kapoor (2017), "What makes sports leagues successful? A study on Indian professional sports leagues, "International Journal of Indian Culture and Business Management, Interscience Enterprises Ltd, Vol. 15(2), pp. 206-228. URL: ps://ideas.repec.org/a/ids/ijicbm/v15y2017i2p206-228.html
- Trivedi, Abhinav (2013), IPL 2013 final match ratings drop by 28 per cent, Exchange4media, June 7, 2013, URL: https://www.exchange4media.com/amp/media-tv-news/ipl-2013-final-match-ratings-drop-by-28-per-cent-51339.html
- USA Today (2019), English Premier League broadcast rights rise to $12 billion, May 21, 2019 URL: https://www.usatoday.com/story/sports/soccer/2019/05/21/english-premier-league-broadcast-rights-rise-to-12-billion/39500789/
- Vasavda, M and Pritam Pal Singh (2020), 54 National Sports Federations lose recognition after High Court Order, Indian Express, New Delhi, June 26, 2020 URL: https://indianexpress.com/article/sports/sport-others/national-sports-federations-lose-recognition-delhi-high-court-order-6476622/
- Vasu, Anand (2019), Is Indian Cricket is better or Worse for what it has gone through since the appointment of CoA a Two year ago, 29 September 2019, Economic Times, URL: https://economictimes.indiatimes.com/news/sports/is-indian-cricket-is-better-or-worse-for-what-it-has-gone-through-since-the-appointment-of-coa-two-year-ago/articleshow/71365822.cms
- Vivek, T R (2011), Business lessons from IPL: Franchise model is risk free, September 14, 2011, Economic Times, URL: https://economictimes.indiatimes.com/news/company/corporate-trends/business-lessons-from-ipl-franchise-model-is-risk-free/articleshow/7930446.cms
- Waris, Sarah (2020), India Open Boxing Championship winners yet to receive prize money, The Bridge, January 11, 2020, URL:https://thebridge.in/boxing/india-open-boxing-championship-winners-receive-prize-money/
- Weekend Team (2013), Beyond Business, IPL or ICL Indian Controversial League, Business Standard, January 20, 2013, URL:https://www.business-standard.com/article/beyond-business/ipl-or-icl-indian-controversial-league-109041800020_1.html
- Wenner Lawrence, A.(2021), Forthcoming, "Media, Sports & Society", Loyola Marymont University and Loyola Law School, URL: https://digitalcommons.lmu.edu/comm_fac/12/

- Wisden India Staff (2012), Sun TV Network win Hyderabad IPL franchise, Wisden India, October 25, 2012, URL: http://www.wisdenindia.com/cricket-news/sun-tv-network-win-hyderabad-ipl-franchise/32100

Web Links

- http://bengalurubulls.com/
- http://bengalwarriors.com/
- http://blog.nielsen.com
- http://dabangdelhi.com/about
- http://jaipurpinkpanthers.com/#/about-us
- http://mib.nic.in/
- http://mumbairockets.net/management/
- http://provolleyball.in
- http://sports.indiapress.org/
- http://sportzlive.net/
- http://www.awadhewarriors.in/
- http://www.bbc.co.uk/worldservice/specials/1157_cricket_history/page6.shtml
- http://www.chennaisuperkings.com
- http://www.deccanchargers.com/
- http://www.hyderabadhunters.com/
- http://www.iccrindia.net/sports/
- http://www.kkr.in/
- http://www.kochituskers.in/
- http://www.kxip.in/
- http://www.mumbaiindians.com/
- http://www.prowrestlingleague.com/
- http://www.punewarriorsindia.com/
- http://www.rajasthanroyals.com/
- http://www.royalchallengers.com/
- http://www.updangal.com/
- https://chennaiyinfc.com/owners/
- https://fcgoa.in/about
- https://globalsportmatters.com
- https://pib.gov.in/newsite/
- https://themohunbaganac.com/management/
- https://www.7acespune.com/
- https://www.bengalurufc.com/owners/
- https://www.fcjamshedpur.com/about-us
- https://www.fortunegiants.com/about-gujarat-fortune-giants

- https://www.haryanasteelers.com/
- https://www.hawkeyeinnovations.com/sports/cricket
- https://www.historyonthenet.com/the-mayan-ball-game
- https://www.indiansuperleague.com/
- https://www.indiapost.com/top-5-biggest-indian-sports-league/
- https://www.kreedon.com/bengaluru-raptors/
- https://www.mehtagroup.com/sports.html
- https://www.mlb.com/
- https://www.nba.com/
- https://www.neufc.com/
- https://www.nfl.com/
- https://www.nhl.com/
- https://www.odishafc.com/
- https://www.olympic.ind.in
- https://www.patnapirates.net/pages/about
- https://www.pbl-india.com/
- https://www.premierleague.com/
- https://www.prokabaddi.com/
- https://www.prokabaddi.com/about-prokabaddi
- https://www.rpsg.in/business#Sports
- https://www.sportanddev.org/
- https://www.sportskeeda.com/
- https://www.statista.com/
- https://www.telugutitans.in/
- https://www.ultimatetabletennis.in/
- https://www.upyoddha.co.in/about-us
- https://www.usports.in/about-team/usports
- https://www.vizrt.com/
- https://yas.nic.in/
- www.delhidaredevils.com/
- www.Economictimes.com
- www.Indiatoday.in
- www.Iplt20.com
- www.socialsamosa.com
- www.Timesofindia.com
- www.business-standard.com/
- https://www.insidesport.co
- https://www.hindustantimes.com
- https://khelnow.com/
- britishesports.org